writers
and their times

Harriet Beecher Stowe

and the
Abolitionist
Movement

Alison Morretta

Cavendish
Square

New York

For Connie

Published in 2015 by Cavendish Square Publishing, LLC
243 5th Avenue, Suite 136, New York, NY 10016

Library of Congress Cataloging-in-Publication Data

Morretta, Alison.
Harriet Beecher Stowe and the Abolitionist Movement / by Alison Morretta.
p. cm. — (Writers and their times)
Includes index.
ISBN 978-1-62712-803-2 (hardcover) ISBN 978-1-62712-805-6 (ebook)
1. Stowe, Harriet Beecher, — 1811-1896 — Juvenile literature. 2. Antislavery movements — United States — History — 19th century — Juvenile literature. 3. Abolitionists — United States — History — 19th century — Juvenile literature. I. Morretta, Alison. II. Title.
PS2956.M67 2015
813—d23

Editorial Director: Dean Miller   Art Director: Jeffrey Talbot
Editor: Kristen Susienka   Designer: Amy Greenan
Copy Editor: Cynthia Roby   Production Manager: Jennifer Ryder-Talbot
Production Editor: David McNamara
Photo Research by J8 Media

Printed in the United States of America

Contents

Introduction

The Little Woman Who Started the Great War

Harriet Beecher Stowe may seem like an unlikely catalyst for the American Civil War (1861–1865), but her bestselling novel, *Uncle Tom's Cabin* (1852), brought the realities of the slave system into the hearts and minds of the average American reader. Many political and economic factors in the early nineteenth century combined to make slavery a controversial topic. However, Stowe presented the question of slavery as a moral issue. By doing so, she started a national dialogue that intensified the existing tensions that ultimately led to war.

A white New Englander from a prominent Protestant family, Stowe was a traditional nineteenth-century woman in many ways. Unlike other female abolitionists at the time, Stowe shied away from public speaking and used her pen to make her voice heard. She believed that the best way for a woman to have influence in a male-dominated society was through moral and spiritual guidance, which was within the traditional domestic sphere assigned to females. A deeply religious woman from

Alanson Fisher painted this portrait of Harriet Beecher Stowe in 1853, the year after the publication of *Uncle Tom's Cabin*.

a family of clergymen, Stowe found the institution of slavery incompatible with her Christian values, as well as with the democratic principles on which the young nation was founded. Though Stowe had her own racial prejudices, she nonetheless believed wholeheartedly that slavery was a moral evil and a stain on America.

The early nineteenth century saw the nation expanding westward and acquiring new territory, and the question of whether states would become slave or free was a major political issue. It was also a time of great religious fervor, with Christian missionaries going west to ensure the spiritual health of the nation. It was a common belief that America needed to be morally purified so that the nation could prepare for the second coming of Christ, as foretold by the Bible. This belief fueled a great deal of social reform. The most egregious social ill was the institution of slavery, but the country was divided along sectional lines, with Southerners overwhelmingly proslavery and Northerners against it. In the Border States, especially Ohio (where Stowe spent many years of her life), things were more complicated, and violence between proslavery and antislavery factions become increasingly common in the mid-1800s.

In the South, slavery was an economic necessity and so deeply ingrained in Southern culture that the idea of abolition was unimaginable. In the North, especially in the states of New England, it was something that existed as a concept, but most people had no firsthand knowledge of the practice. Southerners contended that blacks were better off under the influence of white masters and that most slaveholders treated their slaves humanely. At a time when many white Northerners held racial prejudices and believed that the races were different by nature, this argument was enough to keep them complacent. They were opposed to slavery in theory, but it was easy enough for them to ignore it.

When the Fugitive Slave Act became law in 1850, it brought the Southern institution into the free states, and the abolitionist movement gained momentum. With every American citizen now legally obligated to assist in the capture of escaped slaves, Northerners who were morally opposed to slavery were forced to support it or face legal consequences. It was this more than anything else that prompted Stowe to write *Uncle Tom's Cabin*.

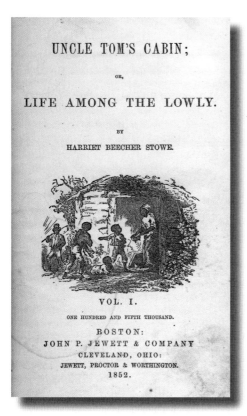

UNCLE TOM'S CABIN;

OR,

LIFE AMONG THE LOWLY.

BY

HARRIET BEECHER STOWE.

VOL. I.

ONE HUNDRED AND FIFTH THOUSAND.

BOSTON:
JOHN P. JEWETT & COMPANY
CLEVELAND, OHIO:
JEWETT, PROCTOR & WORTHINGTON.
1852.

The title page of the first edition of *Uncle Tom's Cabin*.

Especially disturbing to Stowe as a wife and mother was the common practice of separating slave families and selling them to different masters. In *Uncle Tom's Cabin,* she appeals to the white Christian mothers and presents them with the moral dilemmas at the heart of slavery. How can anyone claiming to be a Christian stand by idly while families are torn apart? How can any Christian support a law that forbids them from helping the downtrodden? How can an institution that prohibits the spread of Christianity among slaves be beneficial to a society seeking moral purity? Stowe gives life to a cast of slave characters who have the same yearnings for freedom and salvation, and the same pure, unadulterated love for their families as white people. *Uncle Tom's Cabin* forced the nineteenth-century reader to view things from a different perspective—to see slaves as people and not as property.

The Separation of Mother and Child depicts the slave trader Haley buying a boy and taking him from his mother.

The book was an instant best seller, both in the United States and in Great Britain, and Stowe became the most famous antislavery writer in the nation. The story and its characters became part of American popular culture, with theatrical adaptations reaching even more people than the book. People who would otherwise have ignored the slavery issue were brought over to the antislavery cause either through the reading of the text, listening to the text being read aloud at home (a common practice), or attending one of the many *Uncle Tom* plays put on throughout the nation. The *Uncle Tom* plays are significant not only because of the amount of people they reached, but also because they were some of the first productions to make theater accessible to working-class Americans. As Stowe's story reached an ever-larger audience, more people in the North shed their indifference and became active supporters of the abolitionist movement. On the opposite end, Southerners grew increasingly hostile toward northern abolitionists and antislavery politicians. When Abraham Lincoln was elected president in 1860, it was the last straw for many, and Southern states began to secede from the Union.

When Stowe met Lincoln in 1862, shortly before the Emancipation Proclamation freeing slaves in the Confederate states went into effect, he is reported to have said, "So you're the little woman who wrote the book that started this great war." While Lincoln's initial goal for the Civil War was to keep the Union together, he became increasingly focused on the slavery question at the heart of the divide between North and South. Whether or not the above statement was made, the fact that it has become part of historical lore speaks to the widespread influence *Uncle Tom's Cabin* had on antebellum American attitudes about slavery. While the war was likely inevitable, it is undeniable that Harriet Beecher Stowe, the little white woman from New England, played a major role in shaping the cultural landscape of a nation on the verge of war.

ONE

The Slavery Question in Antebellum America

The movement for the abolition of slavery reached its peak during the mid-nineteenth century, especially in the years leading up to the Civil War. As early as America's colonial period, however, there were individuals who objected to bringing the institution of slavery to the New World. The first slaves were brought to the colony of Virginia in the mid-1600s, when the transatlantic slave trade was active in bringing Africans to the New World. Africans were bought or captured by European slave traders, who sold them to colonists in the Americas. The slave trade was a profitable business for both Europeans and colonists in the process of settling new territory. The democratic ideals that would lead to revolution, however, stood in direct contrast to the "peculiar institution" of slavery. Almost from the beginning, there were individuals who sought to abolish slavery in America.

During the height of the slave trade, native Africans were taken from their homeland and brought to the United States to work on plantations.

Early Abolition Movement

In the colonial era, the largest group to oppose slavery was the Quakers, who had settled mainly in Pennsylvania and Rhode Island. The Quakers' religious beliefs were based on the notion of equality and brotherhood, and they believed that people could achieve salvation through emulating Jesus Christ and doing good works. These ideals clashed with the institution of slavery, in which people were bought and sold and denied their humanity. These individuals, who believed the institution to be unchristian, led the earliest antislavery movement in the Americas.

Thomas Jefferson kept slaves at Monticello, his plantation in Virginia.

The American Revolution (1775–1783) brought the issue of slavery into the public consciousness on different grounds. The war for America's independence from Britain was based on the idea of freedom, and the Declaration of Independence (1776) stated that "all men are created equal" and have a right to "life, liberty, and the pursuit of happiness." While many of the Founding Fathers—including Thomas Jefferson, who drafted the declaration—owned slaves, there were some people in the new republic who believed this declaration should apply to all.

The Northern states abolished slavery between 1777 and 1804, and states in the upper South eased the restrictions on the **manumission**, or voluntary emancipation, of slaves. With the United States expanding west into new territory, the Northwest Ordinance of 1787 banned slavery in the area north of the Ohio River, but did not restrict territory to the south. The economy of the lower South was dependent on slave labor, especially on the growing number of cotton plantations. Also, the people of influence in the region were proslavery.

The Second Great Awakening

By the 1820s, a Protestant religious movement called the "Second Great Awakening" had swept the growing nation. As ministers were sent west to spread Christianity to the new territories, they brought their religious message directly to the people. The Awakening focused on the individual's ability to achieve salvation through free will and the act of being a good Christian through living a moral life.

Also popular at this time was the Protestant theology of **postmillennialism**. This is the belief (according to their interpretation of the Book of Revelation) in the second coming of Christ after the millennium—a golden age of 1,000 years (a figure translated both literally and symbolically) when the Earth has been made morally pure through Christian ethics, allowing for the salvation of nearly all men. This belief was especially relevant to antislavery Christians, who believed that Christ could not return while the moral evil of slavery continued in America. Slavery broke up families and encouraged violence and infidelity. The slave was the property of the master and not of God, and in many cases slaves were not allowed to practice Christianity because they were considered subhuman and without souls to be saved. For many nineteenth-century Christians, therefore, it was a moral imperative to eradicate slavery for the salvation of all mankind.

African Americans board a ship in Savannah, Georgia, in 1895. The ship was bound for the African country of Liberia, which was created as a place to send emancipated slaves.

Antislavery Organizations

William Lloyd Garrison published the abolitionist paper *The Liberator*.

In the early years of the nineteenth century there was more organization in the abolitionist movement. In 1816, the American Colonization Society (ACS) was established. The ACS was an antislavery organization whose members believed in the colonization approach to emancipation: slaves should be freed and sent back to Africa. The group helped to establish the African nation of Liberia, where freed slaves could be sent.

The main abolitionist organization during the mid-nineteenth century was the American Anti-Slavery Society (AASS). Established in 1833 in Philadelphia, Pennsylvania, by William Lloyd Garrison, publisher of the abolitionist newspaper *The Liberator*, and New York businessmen Arthur and Lewis Tappan, the AASS called for the immediate emancipation of slaves without compensation to the slaveholders. This more militant approach to abolition stood in contrast to older notions of the gradual abolition of slavery with restitution to the owners. Garrison and his followers rejected this in favor of aggressive action against the institution of slavery, which they viewed as a moral evil that must not be rewarded.

The AASS also advocated women's rights and allowed female members. This was controversial, as the woman's place was in the home and it was considered improper for women to give public speeches. The issue of women's rights was one of many that split members of the organization, and in 1840 some members (including the Tappans) broke away and formed the American and Foreign Anti-Slavery Society (AFASS). Members of the AFASS believed that the Garrisonian approach to abolition, which attacked the U.S. Constitution and advocated rights for women in addition to racial equality, was too radical. The AASS sought reform through "moral suasion"—seeking change through the moral purification of the people—and rejected the government as corrupt. The AFASS believed that political reform was the only viable way to attack the institution of slavery.

African-American Abolitionists

A number of influential free blacks in the North made significant contributions to the cause through membership in organizations, financial support of existing antislavery publications, and publication of their own abolitionist newspapers and literature. Membership in the AASS was open to African Americans and many prominent black abolitionists became involved in the organization, most notably Frederick Douglass.

Born Frederick Augustus Washington Bailey in Talbot County, Maryland, Douglass escaped bondage in 1838 and settled in Massachusetts. There he became involved in the thriving abolitionist movement in New Bedford, a community of free blacks. Douglass, who had been mostly self-educated, subscribed to *The Liberator* and was asked by the AASS to speak at antislavery meetings. He later began to publish his own newspaper, the *North Star*. His autobiography, *Narrative of the Life of Frederick Douglass* (1845), was a bestseller and remains one of the most important works of literature in American history. It was one of the first slave narratives to contradict the idea that blacks were inherently inferior to whites. Douglass' skill as an orator and a writer, which outshone

Black abolitionist Frederick Douglass was a gifted orator and writer. He published his own memoir, *Narrative of the Life of Frederick Douglass,* in 1845.

the skills of many of his white contemporaries, made him one of the most influential leaders of the abolitionist movement. Douglass provided the public with living proof that African Americans, when given the chance, could become highly educated and productive members of society.

17

Former slave Sojourner Truth became a prominent supporter of both the abolitionist and women's rights movements.

Another important black abolitionist was also a female. Former slave Sojourner Truth, born Isabella Baumfree, escaped bondage in 1826—just one year before New York State banned slavery. With the help of a Quaker family, Truth and her infant daughter escaped Ulster County and settled in New York City. Though she was illiterate, Truth became a devout Christian and had both an extensive knowledge of the Bible and a gift for oratory. She officially changed her name to Sojourner Truth in 1843, when she felt God had given her a calling. She then became active in the abolitionist community in Northampton, Massachusetts. Truth was a proponent of women's rights as well as abolition. While in Northampton she became acquainted with Garrison and Douglass. In 1850, Garrison published her memoirs, *The Narrative of Sojourner Truth: Northern Slave*. Truth also went on speaking tours and preached on the issues of slavery and women's rights. She famously clashed with Frederick Douglass during an abolitionist meeting in 1852 over the issue of a violent response to slavery, asking, "Frederick, is God gone?" Truth continued her humanitarian efforts throughout the Civil War years and into Reconstruction.

Women and the Abolition Movement

Traditionally, women in the nineteenth century were not active in matters of state, as politics was considered the domain of men. A woman's influence was restricted to the domestic sphere. Her purpose was to bear and raise children and to keep the home. Matters of education and religion were, however, in the female sphere. Thus certain social issues, such as **temperance**, were taken up by women who felt that drunkenness led to domestic issues such as abuse, loss of income, and infidelity. Women tended to argue on religious and moral grounds, and many were drawn to the abolitionist cause because they viewed the institution as immoral and unchristian.

Abolitionists Sarah Grimké (left) and her younger sister Angelina (right) went on lecture tours.

The nature of society made it much easier for white women to be active in the abolitionist movement, since it was dangerous for the average black woman to be in the public eye. The Fugitive Slave Act made it legal to pursue and capture escaped slaves. Even free black women ran the risk of a false claim of ownership that would legally require their capture and return to bondage.

Sisters Sarah and Angelina Grimké had firsthand experience of the plight of slaves, having grown up on a South Carolina plantation. Sarah, the elder sister by thirteen years, used to read the Bible to the slaves even though it was illegal to do so. Both she and her sister, Angelina, had become increasingly disturbed by the inequality and injustice of slavery. Sarah Grimké rejected the Episcopalian faith of her youth and became a Quaker when she moved north to Philadelphia. Angelina followed her nine years later, and the sisters became active in the abolitionist movement. Angelina wrote a letter to William Lloyd Garrison that was published (without her permission) in *The Liberator* in

1836. That same year she wrote her first pamphlet, "Appeal to the Christian Women of the South," in which she implored Southern women to join the cause of the abolitionists on moral grounds.

The Grimké sisters broke out of the "woman's sphere" by going on lecture tours and routinely speaking to audiences containing men and women—something almost unheard of at the time. The controversy caused by the fact that they were female public speakers only reinforced their belief in the need for women's rights as well as the abolition of slavery. Like Sojourner Truth, the Grimkés believed that the two issues were related, and that women shared a natural bond regardless of race. The Grimkés were the first female members of the AASS, and spoke and published on the issues of abolition and women's rights.

Angelina Grimké was the first woman to speak before a legislative body when she addressed the Massachusetts legislature in February 1838. Though Angelina was the better public speaker, Sarah was an excellent writer, publishing a series of "Letters on the Equality of the Sexes" (1837) in the *New England Spectator*. Angelina married prominent abolitionist Theodore Weld in 1838. Though Angelina retired from public speaking after a mob burned Philadelphia's Pennsylvania Hall one day after she had given a speech there, she continued to write and work, with her husband and with Sarah, toward racial and gender equality in the United States.

Slavery and the Southern Economy

In 1793, Eli Whitney's cotton gin revolutionized cotton production. Prior to Whitney's invention, cotton was a labor-intensive crop, as the seeds had to be removed by hand. Whitney's cotton gin mechanically separated the seeds from the cotton and increased the speed of production. The profitability of cotton led Southern planters to buy more land, which required more slaves to work it. "King Cotton" became the dominant crop of the South, and by the mid-nineteenth century,

Eli Whitney's cotton gin, which sped up the production process, increased the need for slave laborers to pick cotton in the fields.

cotton was America's leading export. The cotton industry also benefited the North, which had many textile mills that used cotton fiber to manufacture their products.

Slavery was deeply rooted not only in the economy of the South but also in its culture and politics. The aristocratic social structure normalized the concept of servitude—with the landowning class holding all the wealth and power—and made education a privilege reserved for wealthy upper-class whites. Southern slaveholders also used the Bible, which includes instances of slavery, as a rationalization for the institution. They claimed that African Americans were barbaric and were better off under the influence of civilized Christians.

The Scenes which the above Plate is designed to represent—are—Fig. 1, a Mother intreating for the lives of her children.—2, Mr. Travis, cruelly murdered by his own Slaves.—3, Mr. Barrow, who bravely defended himself until his wife escaped.—4, A comp. of mounted Dragoons in pursuit of the Blacks.

Nat Turner Rebellion

On August 21, 1831, a slave and lay preacher named Nathaniel "Nat" Turner (1800–1831) led a rebellion in Southampton County, Virginia. Deeply religious, Turner believed that he had been given a sign from God to attack the institution of slavery through violence. Turner and his men killed the family of Turner's master, Joseph Travis (above). They then went on a killing spree throughout the county, gathering more followers. By the end of the rebellion, Turner's men numbered about sixty, and they had killed fifty-five white Southerners.

The uprising caused widespread fear in the slave states, which enacted harsh laws that made it illegal to teach African Americans (slaves or freedmen) to read and write. They also prohibited religious organizations that didn't have a white minister. Southern supporters of slavery had always insisted that masters were kind to their slaves and that the institution did more good than harm to them. The uprising forced people to confront the fact that the slaves were not content to be held in bondage.

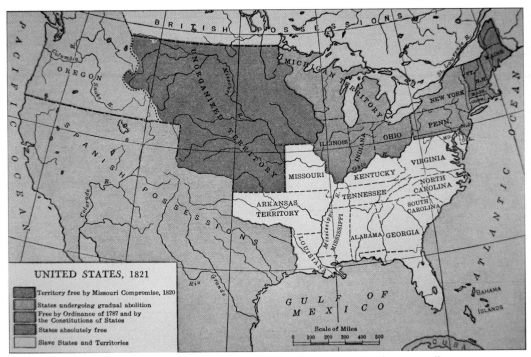

This 1821 map shows the borders established after the Louisiana Purchase, as well as the Missouri Compromise line, which divided the states into free and slave.

Slaveholding white Southern males had great political influence, as for a long time only white male landowners could vote. Southern politicians were in favor of slavery because it pleased their constituents and because it was vital to the region's agrarian economy. Southerners were also generally in favor of states' rights and did not believe it was constitutional for the federal government to regulate slavery. With westward expansion, Southern politicians saw in the new territories potential slave states, which would increase the political power and representation of the South in Congress.

Territorial Expansion

With the acquisition by the United States of territory from France in the Louisiana Purchase of 1803, more land was available for settlement. The Missouri Compromise of 1820 addressed the question of whether the new territories would be admitted to the union as free states or slave states. The Compromise was an agreement between proslavery and antislavery factions in the U.S. Congress to regulate slavery in the west. It prohibited slavery in the portion of the Louisiana Territory north of the 36°30′ parallel, with the exception of the proposed slave state of Missouri. Maine was admitted as a free state to maintain balance in the Union.

This line would later be called into question as the United States continued its policy of imperialistic expansion, known as **manifest destiny**, and more territory was acquired in the western frontier. The desire to spread American values and Christianity westward was a driving force during this period, and led to increased tensions between the North and South.

The Mexican Cession and the Wilmot Proviso

A believer in the concept of manifest destiny, President James K. Polk continued the policy of westward expansion of the U.S. when he took office in 1845. The Republic of Texas had gained its independence from Mexico in 1836, but the United States did not grant statehood largely because Northerners did not want another slave state admitted to the Union. Polk pursued the **annexation** of Texas, and in 1845 it was admitted as the twenty-eighth state.

Polk was not content only with Texas, however. When the offer to purchase the land that is now the southwestern United States was rejected, border clashes broke out in the Rio Grande region. The United States went to war with Mexico in May 1846. Shortly thereafter, Congress went to work on an **appropriations** bill to negotiate the end of the war. An amendment to this bill—known as the Wilmot Proviso—was proposed in the U.S. House of Representatives by Pennsylvania congressman David Wilmot. The amendment sought to ban slavery in any territory acquired from Mexico. Although it did not pass the Senate, the Wilmot Proviso added to the growing hostility between the North and the South and raised the question of whether Congress had the power to regulate slavery.

The Mexican-American war officially ended with the signing of the Treaty of Guadalupe Hidalgo in February 1848. The treaty gave the United States the area known as the Mexican Cession—525,000 square miles (1.4 million sq. km) of territory, including present-day California, Nevada, Utah, most of New Mexico and Arizona, and parts of Wyoming and Colorado. This bred further conflict between the North and South. The new territory under the Missouri Compromise line would allow slavery in much of the newly acquired land.

The Compromise of 1850 and the Fugitive Slave Act

In 1850, after years of sectional conflict in Congress, an agreement was reached regarding handling the new territory. The Compromise of 1850 was an **omnibus bill** that sought to restore harmony to the Union on the question of slavery in the Mexican Cession. Drafted by Kentucky senator Henry Clay and Illinois senator Stephen A. Douglas, the collection of five bills gave Texas compensation for giving up land in New Mexico territory, admitted California into the Union as a free state, left the slavery question in the New Mexico and Utah territories to be determined by inhabitants of the state (a policy known as popular sovereignty), and outlawed the slave trade in Washington, D.C.

The most controversial piece of legislation was the Fugitive Slave Act, which required citizens of both slave and free states to assist in the capture of runaway slaves. It also denied fugitives the right to jury trials. Cases would be handled by federal commissioners, who received more money for returning

John Brown's Raid

Abolitionist John Brown was an insurrectionist who believed in responding to slavery with violence. From October 16 to 18, 1859, he led a raid on the federal arsenal in Harpers Ferry, Virginia. His goal was to seize weapons from the U.S. military arsenal at Harpers Ferry in order to arm the slaves for a rebellion. Brown's men seized hostages and tried to hold the arsenal but were quickly defeated by federal forces. Ten of Brown's men were killed, and Brown himself was wounded. Brown was tried and convicted of treason and murder by the state of Virginia and executed on December 2, 1859. Though the Harpers Ferry raid was a complete failure, it added to Southern fears of slave rebellion and made Brown into a martyr who fueled the Northern abolitionists' cause.

slaves than for freeing them. The act was unpopular among Northerners, who saw it as an extension of slavery into the free states by forcing individuals who were against slavery to violate their beliefs. It added fuel to the abolitionists' cause and increased participation in the Underground Railroad, a network of individuals who covertly helped fugitive slaves avoid capture and escape to freedom in Canada.

Bleeding Kansas

The conflict over slavery turned violent after the passage of the Kansas-Nebraska Act in 1854. Illinois senator Stephen A. Douglas, who wanted to build a transcontinental railroad through the Midwest, proposed the bill. In an attempt to get Southern senators to agree to the bill, he proposed splitting the area into two territories: Nebraska and Kansas. Douglas assumed that the northernmost territory of Nebraska would enter the Union as a free state and Kansas (located next to the slave state of Missouri) would enter as a slave state. But since both lay above the 36°30′ parallel, the act effectively repealed the Missouri Compromise. It left the question of slavery in the territories to popular sovereignty—a pre-Civil War doctrine asserting the right of the people living in a newly organized territory to decide by vote of their territorial legislature whether or not slavery would be permitted there. The act split the Whig Party and added to existing sectional tension between the North and South. It also sparked a period of violence during the settlement of the region, known as "Bleeding Kansas," which lasted from 1855 to 1857.

Proslavery and antislavery individuals flooded into Kansas and fought for control of the territory. Civil conflict broke out within Kansas when the two factions set up separate governments. The Northerners claimed that the proslavery government, recognized by the United States, was a fraud and supporters of slavery known as Border Ruffians had fixed the

Illinois senator Stephen A. Douglas' Kansas-Nebraska Act left the decision on slavery in these new territories to the people, which led to violence between proslavery and antislavery settlers.

election. After Ruffians from Missouri looted the town of Lawrence (which was populated by free-staters), the antislavery faction responded with violence. In May 1856, militant abolitionist John Brown led men into the Pottawatomie Creek area (which was settled by supporters of slavery) and killed five people. This event, known as the Pottawatomie Massacre, sparked months of armed conflict in the region and increased sectional tensions, setting the stage for civil war on a national scale.

The Dred Scott Decision

The final blow to the Missouri Compromise line came in March 1857 with the Supreme Court's decision in *Dred Scott v. Sanford*. Dred Scott, a slave from Missouri who had temporarily resided with his owner in Northern free states,

Abraham Lincoln's Emancipation Proclamation freed Southern slaves during the Civil War. The Thirteenth Amendment (1864) outlawed slavery in America.

sued for freedom for himself and his family after the death of his master. Scott claimed that, since he was living in territory where slavery was illegal, he was no longer a slave. The Supreme Court, under proslavery chief justice Roger B. Taney, ruled that not only was Dred Scott not entitled to his freedom, but that all African Americans, whether slave or free, were not American citizens and therefore could not sue in federal court.

The ruling also addressed the Missouri Compromise—an issue that was not directly before it—and ruled that it was unconstitutional. This meant that the federal government could not regulate slavery in territories acquired after the creation of the United States. The Dred Scott ruling outraged abolitionists and other supporters of the 36°30′ line who felt that the Missouri Compromise was the last thing holding the Union together.

A House Divided and War

On June 16, 1858, while accepting the newly formed Republican Party's nomination for United States senator from Illinois, Abraham Lincoln declared, "a house divided against itself cannot stand. I believe this government cannot endure, permanently, half slave and half free." While on the senatorial campaign trail, Lincoln argued the slavery question with Democratic incumbent Stephen A. Douglas. Lincoln had previously disagreed with Douglas on the Kansas-Nebraska Act, and he continued his opposition to the spread of slavery in the United States in a series of seven debates from August to October 1858. While Lincoln lost the senatorial race, he gained many supporters across the nation and laid the groundwork for his successful presidential run in the election of 1860.

With the Democratic Party split along sectional lines, Republican candidate Abraham Lincoln was elected the sixteenth president of the United States. Before Lincoln was inaugurated, seven Lower South states—South Carolina, Mississippi, Florida, Alabama, Georgia, Louisiana, and Texas—seceded from the Union and formed the Confederacy. South Carolina was the first to secede in 1860, and Fort Sumter in Charleston Harbor became the first battleground of the Civil War that would ultimately end the peculiar institution of slavery in America.

Publicity photos such as this one of Harriet Beecher Stowe were popular collectibles in the mid-1800s.

TWO

The Life of Harriet Beecher Stowe

H arriet Elisabeth Beecher, who would write one of the most influential books in American history, was born on June 14, 1811, in Litchfield, Connecticut, to Presbyterian minister Lyman Beecher and his first wife, Roxana Foote Beecher. Harriet was the sixth living child in the Beecher family, and she, along with other Beecher siblings, would play a prominent role in the abolitionist movement of the mid-nineteenth century.

Family Background and Childhood

When Harriet was just five years old, her mother died of **tuberculosis**. Roxana became a saintly figure in the Beecher household after her death. She was revered as the epitome of pure womanhood and virtue, and this idealized version of Roxana (perpetuated by Lyman Beecher) was a strong influence on Harriet and her siblings. After Roxana's passing, fifteen-year-old Catharine Beecher (the eldest child) took on the role of mother to her seven younger siblings—a role that would

Prominent Protestant clergyman Lyman Beecher was an important influence on his daughter, Harriet.

continue until Harriet was a grown woman. Even after Lyman married his second wife, Harriet Porter, in 1817, Catharine remained the primary maternal influence in the Beecher home.

Lyman Beecher was one of the most important influences in Harriet's life. Reverend Beecher, who was one of the ministers active in the Second Great Awakening, was a deeply religious

man in the Calvinist tradition of Christianity. **Calvinism** is
a strict interpretation of Christianity that stresses the moral
weakness and depravity of humans (believed to be born into
sin), the sovereignty of God, and the idea of **predestination**
(the belief that everything that will happen has already been
determined by God and cannot be changed).

As a parent, Lyman Beecher was mostly concerned with the
state of his children's souls, and placed great importance on
religious conversion. It was in this environment that Harriet
began her informal education. Reverend Beecher also stressed
to his children the importance of social responsibility, believing
that the best way for people to serve God was to take action
against the moral ills of society. These included alcohol abuse
and the spread of slavery in the growing nation. Lyman
Beecher was active in the temperance movement and gave an
antislavery sermon in response to the Missouri Compromise
in 1820. Though not a radical abolitionist, Reverend Beecher
could not reconcile the institution of slavery with the Christian
faith and believed it needed to be purged from society before
the second coming of Christ.

The Beecher home was a house of learning and Lyman's
library was open to all the children, both male and female.
Harriet became an avid reader as a child and listened to
her father instruct her brothers in the art of debate, both
of which formed a solid basis for her formal schooling.
Harriet was provided with another form of education in the
kitchen of her home, where she first came into contact with
African Americans. Harriet was fond of the Beechers' black
servants—kitchen workers Zillah and Rachel Crooke, and
washerwoman Candace—and the conversations she overheard
and participated in influenced the way she viewed African
Americans. From a very young age, Harriet saw them as people
with the same humanity and emotions as she had. When
Harriet's mother died, for example, Candace was as emotionally

distraught by the loss as the family was. This notion of equality was a radical concept at a time when slavery was a firmly established institution in much of the country and racial prejudice was prominent, even in the Northern states.

Harriet spent parts of her childhood at Nutplains, her maternal grandmother's farm in Guilford, Connecticut. It was there that young Harriet learned to appreciate the domestic arts of sewing and painting, and the traditional "woman's work" of keeping a home. She also enjoyed the pastoral beauty of New England, which she would later romanticize in her writings.

Student and Teacher

Harriet's first formal schooling came at Sarah Pierce's Litchfield Female Academy. The academy was one of the first schools in the nation to provide young girls with an education that focused on academic subjects instead of basic domestic skills. Though the minimum age for acceptance was twelve, Harriet was admitted at age eight and showed a great deal of promise as a student, though only in subjects that interested her. She was excellent at composition, but had no skill or interest in arithmetic.

After Catharine Beecher's fiancé, Alexander Fisher (1822), perished in a shipwreck, she decided she would not marry. Instead, Catherine dedicated her life to the education of women, whom she felt were responsible for the moral and educational development of the next generation. In 1823, she started the Hartford Female Seminary in Hartford, Connecticut, with the help of her sister Mary. Thirteen-year-old Harriet was one of her first pupils. The Beecher family's encouragement of knowledge shaped Catharine's view of formal education. She started her school with the goal of providing women with an education in subjects traditionally reserved for men, such as Latin, rhetoric, logic, philosophy, algebra, and physical education, or **calisthenics**.

Catharine Beecher started one of the nation's first academic schools for women, the Hartford Female Seminary.

Catharine pioneered women's educational reform in her shift away from a traditional, domestic curriculum for young women. It was a place where young women studied and prayed together and shared the experience of "republican sisterhood" in an all-female space. There they could "articulate a culture that spoke directly to and from their experience." It was in this environment that Harriet became skilled at articulating her moral and religious beliefs, which she shared with other women through the written word.

While at Hartford, Harriet became one of the school's assistant pupils—a lower-level teaching position that Catharine devised both to spread out the work among the small staff and reinforce the **egalitarian** nature of the institution. After her own conversion in 1825, Harriet helped with the religious education and conversion of her peers at Hartford. She left the school in 1827 and moved to Boston, where Lyman Beecher had taken a ministerial position. However, Harriet was incredibly unsatisfied and grew moody, as there was no real place for an educated young woman in society at that time. She returned to Hartford and continued learning and teaching there.

Harriet found her true calling in the subjects of rhetoric and composition, for which she would one day become famous. Her passion for the subjects was further influenced by a visit from future abolitionist and women's rights advocate Angelina Grimké in 1831. Angelina was a Quaker, and the Society of Friends placed no restrictions on females speaking at meetings. The idea of a female speaking publically was frowned upon in nineteenth century society, especially in the Protestant faith. This introduction to Quakerism showed Harriet that it was possible for women to have a place in the public sphere.

Going West

In the mid-nineteenth century, the United States was expanding west and many ministers went into this frontier territory to spread the Christian faith. Lyman Beecher took a position as president of the Lane Theological Seminary in Cincinnati, Ohio, and Harriet and Catharine, along with many other members of the Beecher family, went west in 1832. For Reverend Beecher and others of his faith, the spread of Christianity to the west was a moral crusade to save the soul of the nation. He felt it was his duty to convert westerners to the Protestant faith and prevent the spread of Catholicism. A fervent anti-Catholic, Lyman believed that "Catholics and infidels have got the start of us … If we gain the West, all is safe; if we lose it, all is lost."

The move expanded Harriet's horizons beyond New England. She took an interest in geography and soon after her arrival in Cincinnati began writing what would be her first published work, *Primary Geography for Children* (1833), which was coauthored by Catharine. She also wrote an essay, "Modern Uses of Language," published in the March 1833 issue of *Western Monthly Magazine*.

Having spent all of her life in the free states of New England, the issue of slavery had always been more of an abstract concept to Harriet. In Ohio, she was confronted with the reality of the institution, as the slave state of Kentucky was just across the Ohio River. In 1833, Harriet visited a Kentucky plantation owned by a friend of her uncle, Samuel Foote. It made such an impression on her that she later used it as the inspiration for Mr. Shelby's plantation in *Uncle Tom's Cabin*.

The Semi-Colon Club

Samuel Foote regularly hosted meetings of the Cincinnati literary society called the Semi-Colon Club, which was open to both men and women. Harriet was invited to join after the publication of *Primary Geography for Children*. She then began to hone her literary skill in the stimulating environment the club provided. The club also provided her with a group of new, likeminded friends. She soon began to feel a sense of community that she had been missing since she left New England.

Harriet developed a writing style called "parlor literature," which was based in the tradition of letter writing—the dominant form of communication in America at the time. Letters from family members were often read aloud to a group

Cincinnati Public Landing by John Casper Wild shows how narrow the boundary was between the free state of Ohio and the slave state of Kentucky.

of family and friends in the parlors of homes. Such letters included many everyday domestic details to keep relatives informed about each other's lives. Many families like the Beechers were spread out across the growing nation, and letter writing was an important way to keep family ties strong.

The Semi-Colon Club met in Samuel Foote's parlor and the members read their contributions aloud. Writing was one of the few respectable ways that a nineteenth-century woman could earn money, and Harriet had a great interest in fiction.

Both her father and her sister Catharine looked down on fiction as a form of literature, but Harriet pursued her passion and worked on many different papers while a member of the club. These early sketches would form the basis for characters, settings, and full-length stories later in her career. Harriet wrote "Uncle Lot," a character sketch of a New England farmer, for the club. It was published in *Western Monthly Magazine* under the title "A New England Sketch" in 1834. It was her first professionally published story, for which she was paid fifty dollars. Harriet would later publish a compilation of her Semi-Colon Club sketches and stories titled *The Mayflower* (1843).

Semi-Colon Club members were intellectual members of Ohio society and included abolitionist and future Chief Justice of the Supreme Court, Salmon P. Chase, *Western Monthly Magazine* editor James Hall, and Biblical scholar Calvin Ellis Stowe and his wife, Eliza. Harriet and Eliza became close friends and, after Eliza's death in 1834, Harriet grew close to Calvin in their shared grief. The two were married in January 1836. Later that year Harriet gave birth to twin daughters, Eliza and Harriet—who was christened "Hattie."

Life in a Battleground State

While Ohio was a free state, the city of Cincinnati (on the free/slave) border, was divided on the issue of slavery. There was conflict among residents, not only between pro- and antislavery factions, but also among the antislavery faction as to the best way to approach abolition. Lyman Beecher believed that colonization was the best approach, but his position on the issue left him vulnerable at the Lane Seminary, where the student body was much more radical. In the "Lane Debates" of 1834, the students argued in favor of immediate abolition and emancipation over colonization. This enraged the school's conservative trustees. The trustees placed what was essentially a "gag rule" on the students, prohibiting abolitionist meetings

The historic Stowe House in Cincinnati, Ohio, where Harriet lived when she wrote *Uncle Tom's Cabin*.

or speeches on campus. The students rebelled and, led by abolitionist Theodore Weld, left Lane for Oberlin College.

Dissension among scholars was nothing compared to the mob violence that broke out in Cincinnati in 1836. In April, abolitionist James G. Birney moved his newspaper, *The Philanthropist*, to Cincinnati and began disseminating abolitionist literature. This angered the proslavery faction in the area. In late July, a proslavery mob, including men from Kentucky, destroyed Birney's press and threw it into the Ohio River. The mob tried to go after Birney, but Salmon P. Chase stopped them. Undeterred, the mob destroyed the homes of several black families.

The Beechers and other antislavery families carried weapons to protect themselves, and a vigilante committee was armed by the mayor and sent to patrol the city. Harriet also used her words as a weapon, taking her pen and writing a fictional "letter" to the editor of the *Cincinnati Journal* (then under the leadership of her brother, Henry Ward Beecher). Harriet used the male **pseudonym** "Franklin" to argue against mob violence and advocate for Birney's right to free speech. By disguising her voice using a male pseudonym, Stowe legitimized her argument for the paper's audience. She was not as radical when it came to women's rights as were Angelina and Sarah Grimké, who broke from traditional gender roles by speaking in public against slavery. Harriet preferred to stay within the woman's sphere of writing, and early on was hesitant to publish under her own name.

A Complicated Relationship

The economic recession that began with the Panic of 1837 hit the nation hard, and though the Stowes did not lose that much, it was necessary for Harriet to continue writing to bring in income. In order to have time to work, Harriet hired servants to help with her young children and other domestic duties. The Beechers had always had servants while Harriet was growing up and she was accustomed to there being help in the home.

There was a social hierarchy to servants that reflected the prejudices of the time, with "old-stock" immigrants from northern Europe at the top, followed by other white immigrants, and finally African Americans. Despite her abolitionist stance, Stowe displayed some of the prejudice of her time when she hired an English girl as nanny and a German girl for housework. Stowe had a complicated relationship with her servants. While she treated them well and considered them (especially her nanny, Anna Smith) part of the family, there was still a very clear social hierarchy, and Harriet was at the top.

In 1839, the Stowes employed a black servant girl from across the river in Kentucky. At the time, it was not uncommon for slave owners to claim ownership of black men and women residing in free states, especially in the Border States. Despite the fact the Stowes' servant was legally a free woman, the courts often sided with the supposed "masters." When the Stowes

The home of Quakers Levi and Catharine Coffin in the Walnut Hills area of Cincinnati (pictured in 1905) was a stop on the Underground Railroad.

received word that a man claiming to be their servant's former master was coming to claim her, they helped her to flee. Armed to protect themselves, Calvin Stowe and Henry Ward Beecher drove the unnamed girl to the cabin of John Van Zandt—one of Ohio's many stops on the Underground Railroad network of abolitionists—and she was able to escape. The incident appears in detail in *Uncle Tom's Cabin*. The fact that Stowe appropriated the girl's story for her novel in addition to using her as "a labor-saving device" in her home also speaks to the nature of the social relationship between white employers and their black servants.

Working Mother

As was common for women in the nineteenth century, Harriet gave birth to many children in quick succession (with a few miscarriages in between). After the birth of twins Eliza and Hattie in 1836, Harriet gave birth to four more children: Henry Ellis Stowe (1838), Frederick William Stowe (1840), Georgiana May Stowe (1843), and Samuel Charles Stowe (1848). Having five pregnancies in twelve years while performing domestic duties left Harriet exhausted and in poor health. She was sometimes even confined to her bed for long periods.

Harriet pushed herself physically and continued to write regularly during this period, both for the necessary income it brought and because she felt it was her true calling. The Stowes' domestic servants made her work possible, especially Anna Smith, who cared for the young Stowe children while Harriet was too busy or physically unable to do so. Harriet continued to contribute regularly to *Western Monthly Magazine*, began publishing morality stories (especially temperance tales) in the *New-York Evangelist*, and domestic parlor-style stories in the popular women's magazine *Godey's Lady's Book*. This last publication brought her a large readership and allowed her to address an audience that would feature prominently in *Uncle Tom's Cabin*: the American mother.

Tragedy and Rebirth

The 1840s was a difficult period for the Beecher and Stowe families. In 1843, Harriet's brother George shot and killed himself in his backyard. The family maintained it was an accidental death, but Stowe biographer Joan D. Hedrick suggests it was suicide. The religious expectations of the age, especially the doctrine of **perfectionism**, placed a great deal of stress on those who sought to be good Christians. The idea that one could achieve complete spiritual purity before the second coming of Christ caused many people to become **scrupulous**, and Hedrick suggests that George Beecher's preoccupation with Christian perfection led him to take his own life.

Harriet was devastated by George's death, and it caused her to question her own faith. It was hard to reconcile the grief and mourning over a loved one's death with the complete submission to God's will that her religion required. Feeling helpless in the face of death and the growing violence in society, Harriet rejected perfectionism and experienced a rebirth. She believed that the best way to be a good Christian and live a moral life was to try to emulate the actions and beliefs of Jesus Christ.

In 1845, Harriet witnessed a slave auction in Kentucky, where she saw a family torn apart. As was common practice, the husband, wife, and their children were sold to different masters. Harriet, who placed great importance on family—especially the relationship between mother and child—was horrified and deeply affected. The incident fueled her abolitionist writings. She wrote of it in her short story "Immediate Emancipation," published in the January 1845 issue of the *New-York Evangelist*.

Before the advent of modern sanitation, **cholera** epidemics were common in American cities and Harriet came down with the disease in 1845. Though she recovered, the Stowes lost their infant son Samuel to cholera in 1849. At a time when so many mothers lost their infant children to disease, it was common to have a photograph of the deceased taken as a memorial. A post-mortem **daguerreotype** of Samuel Charles Stowe was taken, and the image would be replicated almost exactly in *Uncle Tom's Cabin*.

A Vision from God

A number of forces combined at the beginning of the 1850s that put Harriet on the road to writing her most famous and influential novel. The Stowes moved to Brunswick, Maine, where Calvin had taken a position at Bowdoin College. Soon after their arrival, the Fugitive Slave Act, part of the Compromise of 1850, was made law. Under this act, residents of free states were required to assist in the capture of escaped slaves. The law essentially brought slavery into the free states of the North and outraged abolitionists. Harriet wrote a response in the form of a **parable**, "The Freeman's Dream," published on August 1, 1850 in the *National Era*, an abolitionist newspaper edited by Gamaliel Bailey.

Shortly after the passage of the Fugitive Slave Act, Harriet experienced a vision while at church. Instead of Christ on the cross, she saw a slave being whipped—a scene that she would use in her description of the fate of Uncle Tom. She was inspired by the experience and drew on all available accounts from fugitive slaves and stories from her own servants for material for her antislavery novel. She corresponded with Frederick Douglass, who had escaped bondage to become a prominent abolitionist, and modeled the character of George Harris after him. Fugitive slave Josiah Henson would be the model for Tom, the novel's hero. All of her own life's experiences, as well as those she learned through her research, were combined into *Uncle Tom's Cabin, or, Life Among the Lowly*, which was published serially in the *National Era* from June 1851 to April 1852. It was published as a two-volume book on March 20, 1852, and was an instant bestseller in both the United States and Great Britain.

Uncle Tom's Cabin was almost required reading across the nation. And though it brought Stowe international fame and money, it caused a violent reaction against her in the South. Despite the fact that she attempted to humanize the slave owners in the novel, Southerners rejected the story as abolitionist propaganda filled with lies and exaggerations. In response, Stowe published *A Key to Uncle Tom's Cabin* (1853), in which she includes documentation to back up the claims made in her book. The novel put the question of slavery at the forefront of the American public's consciousness.

European Tour

The Stowes moved to Andover, Massachusetts, in 1853 when Calvin was offered a job at the Andover Theological Seminary. Soon after, a British antislavery society invited Harriet on a speaking tour of Britain and Europe and she sailed for England with Calvin and her brother, Charles, as male escorts. She was given a royal welcome by the British people, whose own antislavery efforts had resulted in the abolishment of slavery in the United Kingdom in 1833. Calvin and Charles spoke for Harriet at the engagements throughout the tour not only because Harriet had stage fright, but also the proscription against females speaking publically would have made it controversial for her to speak for herself.

More than half a million women had signed a petition: "An Affectionate and Christian Address of Many Thousands of Women of Great Britain and Ireland to Their Sisters the Women of the United States of America." The document was bound in twenty-six volumes and presented to Harriet at Dunrobin Castle in Scotland, the home of the Duchess of

A twenty-six volume petition was presented to Harriet Beecher Stowe at the home of the Duchess of Sutherland, Harriet Sutherland-Leveson-Gower.

Sutherland. On her first European tour, Harriet also received what was called the "Penny Offering" from various British supporters. Since Harriet received no royalties for sales of *Uncle Tom's Cabin* in Britain, she was gifted around $20,000 to be used as she saw fit. Her travels abroad provided her with material for a travel guide, *Sunny Memories of Foreign Lands* (1854), which was popular with travelers and provided a cultural context for Americans visiting Europe.

Bleeding Kansas and Dred

When congressman Stephen A. Douglas introduced a bill that would open the new territories of Kansas and Nebraska to the possibility of slavery, with the issue to be decided by popular sovereignty, the abolitionists were enraged. In response, Harriet wrote "An Appeal to the Women of the Free States of America,

Proslavery Border Ruffians crossed from Missouri into Kansas to intimidate or harm voters.

On the Present Crisis in Our Country," which was published in the *Independent* in January 1854. The period of violence that followed the passage of the Kansas-Nebraska Act in 1854, known as "Bleeding Kansas," inspired Harriet to take to her pen and write her third antislavery book, *Dred: A Tale of the Great Dismal Swap* (1856).

Dred, the novel's title character, is based on both Denmark Vesey and Nat Turner. Vesey planned a slave rebellion in 1822, but his plans were leaked and it did not materialize. Turner led a violent rebellion in 1831. The book was a bestseller in America and, on top of the success of *Uncle Tom's Cabin*, Harriet became the most well-known author in the nation. She was still widely hated in the South, and Southerners continued to criticize her for what they claimed were false accusations about the realities of slavery. Unlike *Uncle Tom's Cabin*, in which Stowe presented most Southerners as sympathetic people forced to deal with the horrors of the institution, Dred was a direct and militant attack on the institution of slavery and the Southern judicial system.

An Accidental Drowning

In 1857, Harriet's son Henry Ellis Stowe drowned in the Connecticut River while swimming with his friends from Dartmouth College. At the time of his death, Henry had not experienced his religious conversion, and Harriet worried herself to illness at the thought that he may not be with God in death. Harriet found no comfort in the church, as she felt a disconnect between the detached male ministers and the raw emotion felt by women in mourning.

Harriet had been writing consistently for *The Atlantic Monthly*, and in 1858 the magazine began publishing *The Minister's Wooing* in serial form. It was published in book form in 1859. The novel was Harriet's answer to the patriarchal structure of the Protestant clergy, which she had found so problematic after the loss of Henry. Set in her childhood home of New England, *The Minister's Wooing* presents women as the keepers of spiritual and moral influence. Unable to find solace in the church, the character Mrs. Marvyn, who believes that her son James was lost at sea, is comforted only by Candace, a former slave, who serves as a lay preacher to the grieving Mrs. Marvyn. In this way, Stowe was able to demonstrate that the most effective spiritual leadership comes from women, who understand the struggle between submitting to God's will and the idea of predestination, and mourning the loss of a loved one. It would not be long before Harriet rejected the Calvinism of her father and became an Episcopalian.

Secession and the War Years

Shortly after Abraham Lincoln was elected president in 1860, some of the Southern states seceded from the Union. The Civil War officially began with the attack on Fort Sumter

The American Civil War started with *The Bombardment of Fort Sumter*, in Charleston Harbor, South Carolina.

in Charleston Harbor, South Carolina, in April 1861. Harriet visited Washington, D.C. in November 1862 and spent Thanksgiving with former slaves who had joined Union forces. It was during this visit that Abraham Lincoln is reported to have said, "So you're the little woman who wrote the book that started this great war." While there were many other factors that led to the Civil War, it's clear *Uncle Tom's Cabin* brought the crucial issue of slavery into the hearts and minds of the people.

Harriet was disturbed by the fact that the British, who relied on Southern cotton, did not come out against the Confederacy. She began a reply to the "Affectionate Christian Address" that she had received from the British abolitionists, criticizing the

British response to the American Civil War. It was published as "The Reply" in the January 1863 issue of *Atlantic Monthly*. Lyman Beecher died around the same time "The Reply" was published.

Calvin Stowe retired from Andover soon after Lyman's death and the Stowes moved to Hartford, Connecticut. Their son Frederick had enlisted in the Union army at the beginning of the war and was wounded in the Battle of Gettysburg in July 1863. After his discharge, he became dependent on alcohol, which worried his mother, who was a supporter of temperance. The war ended in 1865, and the following year the Stowes purchased a plantation in Florida, where they employed former slaves and spent winters in the warm climate. They hoped that Frederick would be able to break his alcohol habit if they put him in a managerial position, but he failed. With Frederick's alcoholism only getting worse, the Stowes were then forced to institutionalize him. Frederick struggled with alcoholism for the rest of his life. In 1870 he boarded a ship in San Francisco and was never heard from again.

The Byron Controversy

During her travels abroad, Harriet had befriended Lady Byron, the widow of the great poet Lord Byron. Lady Byron had shared the story of her marriage with Harriet in confidence, but after Lord Byron's mistress published a memoir in 1869 that attacked Lady Byron's character, Harriet made a controversial decision. She wrote "The True Story of Lady Byron's Life," published by *Atlantic Monthly* in August 1869, and for the first time the marriage was presented from the female perspective.

Harriet challenged the image of Lady Byron as cold and calculating, which had been accepted for many years, and told the story that Lady Byron had kept a secret throughout her marriage: Lord Byron had engaged in an incestuous relationship with his half-sister, Augusta Leigh. Harriet followed the article

For a vivid description of ST. AUGUSTIN...

FLORIDA, THE LAND OF FLO...

ooks the whole country for miles and miles around. rom, there:

efore him, in plantation after plantation, a map of the life to v

hing.

saw the d

long row

grounds o

would be

he maste

with the

who had

rations fo

he chirru

the cane

d groani

one by fo

uch a cas

not write

dged by e

strange,

-bale, an

, traces out its promises? Having learned late in life, Tom was

assed on laboriously from verse to verse. Fortunate for him w

ntent on was one which slow reading cannot injure, -- nay, on

s of gold, seem often to need to be weighed separately, that th

priceless value. Let us follow him a moment, as, pointing to e

The Stowes purchased a former plantation in Mandarin, Florida, near Jacksonville, where they spent their winters.

with a book, *Lady Byron Vindicated* (1870). As expected, she was harshly criticized for writing on such a scandalous subject and her assertions were discounted, both for lack of tangible proof and because she was a woman.

Lady Byron (Anne Isabella Noel Byron) was the subject of a controversial book.

The Years that Followed

After the Byron controversy and Frederick's disappearance, Harriet suffered another blow when her brother, Henry Ward Beecher, became involved in a scandal. Henry was accused of committing adultery with the wife of his friend, Theodore Tilton. The Beecher-Tilton scandal of 1870 caused a rift in the family. Harriet supported Henry. However her half-sister, Isabelle, who was active in the women's suffrage movement, was against him. Henry was declared innocent of all charges, but his reputation was hurt by the scandal.

With her life and family in chaos, Harriet threw herself into her work. In 1871 she published two books: *My Wife and I* and *Pink and White Tyranny*. Both were explorations of nineteenth-century attitudes about a woman's role in society. The following year saw the publication of *Oldtown Fireside Stories*, a collection of regional New England sketches in the same vein as her earlier book, *Oldtown Folks* (1869), which she based on Calvin's childhood in Natick, Massachusetts. *Palmetto Leaves*, based on her experiences living in Florida, was published in 1873. Stowe documented life in Florida as well as her attempt to start a church and school to educate free blacks in the region. The book is considered to be the first travel guide to Florida and stimulated tourism in the state.

Stowe turned back to the subject of women in *Woman in Sacred History* (1874), in which she fictionalizes the stories of biblical heroines. She drew on her own religious knowledge as well as that of her husband. As a biblical scholar who had published his own bestseller, *Origin and History of the Books of the Bible* (1867), Calvin was a great help to his wife on this topic. Stowe published a book every year during the 1870s until ending her decades-long publishing career with *Poganuc People* (1878), an autobiographical New England novel about her childhood in Litchfield, Connecticut.

Harriet's health began to decline after Calvin's death in 1886, and the deaths of her brother, Henry, and daughter, Georgiana, the following year. She displayed signs of dementia, rewriting *Uncle Tom's Cabin* as if for the first time and going through periods of diminished mental capacity. Harriet Beecher Stowe died at her Hartford home on July 1, 1896, surrounded by family.

Life on the plantations was nowhere near as idealized as this engraving of a slave mother watching over her children at play.

THREE

Uncle Tom's Cabin

A fter serialization in *The National Era* magazine from 1851 to 1852, Harriet Beecher Stowe's *Uncle Tom's Cabin, or, Life Among the Lowly* was published in book form on March 20, 1852. Written in the parlor style, which was meant to be read aloud in homes, the book reached a large audience, both in the North and South. Though many people, especially Southerners, criticized the book for its **sentimentalism** and questioned its accuracy, Stowe's antislavery novel brought the horrors of slavery into the homes and minds of people for whom the institution was more a concept than a reality.

Plot Summary

The story opens on a Kentucky plantation, with slaveholder Arthur Shelby negotiating with Haley, a slave trader. Shelby is a "man of humanity" but is forced to sell slaves to pay off his debts. He suggests that the trader buy Tom, who is an honest, pious man, but Haley says the price is too high. A child named Harry enters the room and Shelby has him perform for Haley.

The boy's mother, a beautiful young **mulatto** woman named Eliza Harris, comes to fetch him. Haley insists that Shelby sell him Harry along with Tom. Shelby is hesitant to separate mother and child, but his debts outweigh his doubts.

Eliza, Mrs. Shelby's housemaid, has overheard their conversation and gone to her mistress with her concerns. Emily Shelby, a woman of "high religious and moral sensibility," believes that her husband would not do such a thing and reassures Eliza that Harry will not be taken from her.

Eliza is married to George Harris, a mulatto slave who works on a nearby plantation. George was hired out by his master to work at a factory, where he designed a machine for cleaning hemp that "displayed quite as much mechanical genius as Whitney's cotton gin." George's master disapproves of his ingenuity and relegates him to manual labor on his estate. With her husband away most of the time due to his new labor schedule, and with memories of losing two children to miscarriage, Eliza is especially attached to her only child.

Despondent over the horrible situation in which his master has placed him, George comes to visit his family and tells Eliza that he plans to escape. Eliza, who is a devout Christian, pleads with George not to go and tells him that he should trust in God. But George is determined to seek his freedom. Because the law does not recognize slave marriages, his master plans to marry him to another woman. His love for Eliza and their son will not allow him to accept this fate. George does not share Eliza's faith and cannot trust in any god that would allow him to suffer as he does. He vows to make it to Canada and purchase freedom for his wife and child. "I'll be free, or I'll die!" he tells Eliza.

At Uncle Tom's cabin, Tom's wife, Chloe—the Shelbys' cook—is preparing dinner for her family. During the flurry of domestic activity, Tom is with the Shelbys' son, George, who is teaching him to write. Young "Mas'r George" eats with the

A black slave and lay preacher delivers a sermon in a meeting much like the ones that Tom held in his cabin.

family and has a friendly relationship with them, despite the fact that they are slaves. Tom, who is the "patriarch in religious matters" to the other slaves, leads a prayer meeting in his cabin.

During this pious and domestic scene, Mr. Shelby is finalizing the sale of Tom and Harry to the slave trader. Mrs. Shelby is horrified and tries to convince him not to go through with the sale. As a Christian woman, Mrs. Shelby tried to do right by the "poor, simple, dependent creatures" and taught them "the duties of the family, of parent and child, and husband and wife." She sees slavery as a sin—"a curse to the master and a curse to the slave"—and is disheartened to learn that, even though she tried to give them the best life that she could, she is powerless against the institution of slavery, which makes the sale of people an economic necessity.

Eliza decides she must flee rather than be separated from her only child. She takes Harry to Uncle Tom's cabin and informs them of the sale. Aunt Chloe pleads with Tom to go with Eliza but he refuses, still believing in his master's goodness and refusing to break his trust. He then cries over the bed of his children.

When Mrs. Shelby discovers that Eliza and Harry have gone, she is thankful. Mr. Shelby is more concerned with the fact that Haley might believe he had aided Eliza in her escape. When Haley arrives, Mr. Shelby provides him with a horse to go after Eliza, but the slaves conspire to make it difficult for him to catch up to her. The Shelbys are aware of what is happening but do not stop it, and Mrs. Shelby helps them by insisting Haley stay for lunch.

The story then backtracks to Eliza's escape. She is on foot and carrying Harry, and though the journey is long she is able to overcome the physical struggle, for "stronger than all was maternal love." The slave state of Kentucky is just across the Ohio River from the free state of Ohio, and when Eliza reaches the border town, "her first glance was at the river, which lay, like Jordan, between her and the Canaan of liberty on the other side." The river is frozen so Eliza, whose skin is so light that she could pass for a white woman, takes a room at an inn and waits.

Back at the Shelby plantation, Aunt Chloe is taking her time preparing the food to further delay Haley. Talking to Tom and her children, she curses the trader, but the ever-pious Tom urges her to pray for the man, telling her he would "rather be sold, ten thousand times over, than have all that ar poor crittur's got to answer for." When the search party finally leaves, slaves Andy and Sam are sent to lead Haley and take him on the incorrect route to buy more time for Eliza. They eventually

The image of Eliza escaping across the Ohio River became iconic after the publication of *Uncle Tom's Cabin*.

$200 Reward.

RANAWAY from the subscriber, on the night of Thursday, the 30th of Sepember.

FIVE NEGRO SLAVES,

To-wit : one Negro man, his wife, and three children.

The man is a black negro, full height, very erect, his face a little thin. He is about forty years of age, and calls himself *Washington Reed*, and is known by the name of Washington. He is probably well dressed, possibly takes with him an ivory headed cane, and is of good address. Several of his teeth are gone.

Mary, his wife, is about thirty years of age, a bright mulatto woman, and quite stout and strong.

The oldest of the children is a boy, of the name of FIELDING, twelve years of age, a dark mulatto, with heavy eyelids. He probably wore a new cloth cap.

MATILDA, the second child, is a girl, six years of age, rather a dark mulatto, but a bright and smart looking child.

MALCOLM, the youngest, is a boy, four years old, a lighter mulatto than the last, and about equally as bright. He probably also wore a cloth cap. If examined, he will be found to have a swelling at the navel.

Washington and Mary have lived at or near St. Louis, with the subscriber, for about 15 years.

It is supposed that they are making their way to Chicago, and that a white man accompanies them, that they will travel chiefly at night, and most probably in a covered wagon.

A reward of $150 will be paid for their apprehension, so that I can get them, if taken within one hundred miles of St. Louis, and $200 if taken beyond that, and secured so that I can get them, and other reasonable additional charges, if delivered to the subscriber, or to THOMAS ALLEN, Esq., at St. Louis, Mo. The above negroes, for the last few years, have been in possession of Thomas Allen, Esq., of St. Louis.

WM. RUSSELL.

ST. LOUIS, Oct. 1, 1847.

It was common for slave owners to place ads in the newspaper and distribute flyers offering a reward for the capture of escaped slaves.

catch up with her and Sam, seeing Eliza at the inn, makes a commotion to warn her. In one of the most iconic scenes in the novel, Eliza, "nerved with strength such as God gives only to the desperate" braves the icy Ohio River, jumping from floe to floe with her child in her arms. (A floe is a sheet or mass of floating ice.) When Eliza reaches Ohio, a man named Mr. Symmes helps her up the bank. Although in violation of the law, he helps her escape to a safe house. Mr. Symmes does not believe he should "be hunter and catcher for other folks."

In Ohio, Senator Bird and his wife debate the recently passed Fugitive Slave Law. Mrs. Bird, who would not normally concern herself with political matters, is outraged by the law, which she views as unchristian. She appeals to her husband on religious grounds, telling Senator Bird, "I don't know anything about politics, but I can read my Bible; and there I see that I must feed the hungry, clothe the naked, and comfort the desolate." Mrs. Bird chastises her husband, who voted in favor of the law, and questions him as to whether he would actually be able to follow the law himself.

Soon after, Mr. Symmes arrives at the Birds' with Eliza and Harry, and Senator Bird's convictions are tested. Eliza appeals to Mrs. Bird on behalf of her son and the children she had lost, and Mrs. Bird (who had just lost a child) takes pity on Eliza and promises to help her. Senator Bird is moved that his "idea of a fugitive was only an idea of the letters that spell the word" and that "he had never thought that a fugitive might be a hapless mother, a defenseless child." He breaks the law he voted for and helps Eliza to a safe house owned by former Kentucky slaveholder John Van Trompe, who moved to Ohio and freed his slaves after realizing that slavery was morally wrong.

Haley has returned to the Shelby plantation to take Tom, who is put in restraints and driven away. Young George, who had been away with a friend and unaware of Tom's sale, catches up with them and Tom urges him to be a good son and a good Christian. George swears that when he is a grown man, he will never own slaves and that he is ashamed to be a Kentuckian, having seen the evils of slavery.

George Harris arrives at a Kentucky inn and his light skin allows him to pass for a Spanish man. There is a sign that announces his escape and describes his appearance and the branded "H" on his hand, but he goes unrecognized by everyone except for Mr. Wilson, the man who owns the factory where George used to work. Mr. Wilson is "divided between his wish to help George, and a certain confused notion of maintaining law and order," but he does not reveal George's identity.

Tom, who has always been an honest, law-abiding man, is forced to spend the night in jail while waiting for the slave auction the next morning. Haley acquires several more slaves at the auction, yet refuses to purchase a mother together with her last remaining son. He then prepares to travel south by boat. The slaves are below deck and the white travelers are above. Meanwhile, human trafficking continues on the boat—Haley sells a woman's infant son to another man, stealing the boy away while he is sleeping. During the night, the grieving woman jumps overboard and kills herself. Stowe addresses the reader and points to the hypocrisy of the attitude toward the slave trade in America: "Trading Negroes from Africa, dear reader, is so horrid! It is not to be thought of! But trading them from Kentucky, —that's quite another thing!"

Eliza has arrived at the home of Quakers Simeon and Rachel Halliday, who take her in and provide for her while she waits to make her next move toward freedom. They learn that Eliza's husband, George, is on his way to the Quaker settlement and the family is reunited that night. The next morning, the Hallidays sit on equal terms with the Harrises at the breakfast table and George realizes for the first time what it means to have a home. His faith is stirred in the presence of the Hallidays' kindness and "a belief in God, and trust in his providence, began to encircle his heart."

On the boat down the Mississippi River, Tom meets a young child named Eva St. Clare. Tom sees an angelic innocence in Eva, who is kind to him and tells him that she will get her father to buy him. When Eva falls overboard, Tom jumps in the river and saves her life. Eva's father, Augustine St. Clare, then agrees to purchase Tom.

Accompanying the St. Clares on the trip south is Augustine's cousin, Ophelia. She is a traditional New England woman

The Underground Railroad, painted by Charles T. Webber, depicts Levi and Catherine Coffin, on whom Simeon and Rachel Halliday are based, helping fugitive slaves.

and has agreed to move in with the St. Clares in New Orleans to help bring order to the household. Ophelia has her own prejudices, and when she sees Eva shaking hands and kissing the black servants, it "turn[s] her stomach." St. Clare's wife, Marie, is a self-centered woman who treats the family's slaves as subhuman—"the idea that they had either feelings or rights had never dawned upon her."

Where Eva does not discriminate in her love for everyone, white or black, in the St. Clare household, Marie does not believe that her slaves are capable of the same thoughts or emotions as white people. While discussing their "degraded race" with Ophelia, Marie is shocked that her husband could compare her feelings to those of a slave's: "Mammy couldn't have the feelings that I should. It's a different thing altogether … as if Mammy could love her dirty little babies as I love Eva!" Despite her prejudices, Ophelia believes that it is the responsibility of whites to educate their slaves and treat them "like immortal creatures, that you've got to stand before the bar of God with." St. Clare later points out Ophelia's Northern hypocrisy. Eva is the "only true democrat" in the family, and she bonds with Tom over their shared faith and love of the Bible. They have a symbiotic relationship: Eva helps Tom to read the Bible, and Tom helps her to understand it.

Eliza and George prepare to leave the Quaker settlement as the slave catcher Tom Loker and his mob are closing in on them. They set off with the Hallidays and camp in a strategic area, protected by a very small gap between two rocks. When the slave catchers arrive, George makes his "declaration of independence," telling the men that he will fight for his liberty or die trying. The men shoot at George and his group, and when Loker approaches them through the narrow pass, George shoots and wounds him. The other slave catchers give up and Eliza takes pity on Loker. The group takes him to a Quaker doctor before continuing on their journey. Eventually, George and Eliza make their way to Canada. Their boat finally reaches the "blessed English shores … with one touch to dissolve every incantation of slavery," and they are free.

At the St. Clare household, a slave woman named Prue comes selling hot rolls. Having become an alcoholic to combat her misery, she is despondent and wishes she were dead. When Tom attempts to dissuade her from drinking, which he believes is a moral evil, she shares with him her background. Prue had been sold into sexual slavery and used by her masters to breed children, who were then sold away from her. Prue's last remaining child died of starvation because her mistress would not give her time away to tend to him. Tom later tells Prue's story to Eva, who is disturbed and saddened by it. Not long after, the family learns that Prue has been whipped to death by her master.

Ophelia and St. Clare debate the slavery question in the wake of Prue's death. St. Clare feels in his heart that slavery is wrong, but the nature of the Southern institution is such that "a man of honorable and humane feelings" can only "shut his eyes all he can, and harden his heart." St. Clare's mother, who was a deeply religious woman, made a deep impression on him during his youth and gave him a moral code that affects the way he views slavery and how he treats his own slaves.

St. Clare buys a young slave named Topsy for Ophelia to educate. When he presents Topsy to her, he makes her do a song and dance. Ophelia does not want her but St. Clare notes her hypocrisy, telling her that she and Christians like her will send missionaries to do good work but are unwilling to do it themselves. Ophelia takes Topsy on, and when she sees that the child's back is scarred from whippings, the "ineffaceable marks of the system under which she had grown up thus far," Ophelia's "heart became pitiful within her." Topsy is a poorly behaved child and she steals from Ophelia, believing that she is "mighty wicked … [and] can't help it." Only words of kindness from Eva—the first display of affection Topsy has ever received—seem to make any impression on the unmanageable child. Yet Topsy is confused by Eva's kindness.

The story jumps ahead two years, with Tom settled in with the St. Clares. Tom and Eva have grown incredibly close and spend a great deal of time together. When the St. Clares go to their villa on the lake, Eva and Tom spend time together in the garden reading the Bible and singing hymns. Tom begins to notice that Eva is looking a bit sickly. Eva points to the heavens and tells Tom that she will soon be going there. When St. Clare's brother, Alfred, visits with his son, Henrique, Eva

"UNCLE TOM'S CABIN."

On her deathbed, Eva implores the slaves to be good Christians.

witnesses her cousin strike his slave, Dodo. She is appalled by the incident and makes Henrique promise to be loving and kind to his servants as the Bible instructs.

Eva's health continues to decline and Marie, who has always been an absentee mother, is more concerned with the effects Eva's illness has on her own health and mental state than she is with her daughter. Eva is kind and cheerful despite her sickness and tells Tom that she understands why Jesus accepted his death. Eva claims she would be happy to die if it could "stop all the misery" experienced by the slaves. Confronting her own mortality, she is more concerned about what will happen to Tom and the other slaves if her father dies. She asks St. Clare to free the slaves, as she would have done, and he promises Eva he will free Tom after she dies.

Despite Ophelia's efforts, Topsy continues to misbehave and Ophelia complains that she can no longer manage the child. Eva overhears this conversation and takes Topsy aside to ask her to be good. Topsy tells Eva that Ophelia cannot even bear to touch her because she is black, and Eva responds by putting her hand on Topsy's shoulder and telling her that she loves her and that Jesus loves her, too. Topsy is moved by this and tells Eva she will be good. Ophelia, who has overheard this, is ashamed of her prejudice and believes she could learn a great deal from Eva, though she is just a child.

On her deathbed, Eva asks for all the slaves to gather around so she can give them each a lock of her hair. She begs them to be good Christians so that she will see them all one day in heaven. After they leave, she pleads with her father to do the same. She dies peacefully in her bed, joyous to be joining her God in heaven. Marie grows even more hysterical and selfish after Eva's death. The slaves are unable to mourn for Eva because Marie requires constant attention. St. Clare is in a state of shock and unable to cry, and Tom watches over him in his grief, and "there was more sorrow to Tom in that still, fixed,

Eva helped Tom learn how to read.

tearless eye, than in all Marie's moans and lamentations."
Tom tries to get St. Clare to embrace God, but he is unable
to find any faith. Only when he listens to Tom's prayer does
St. Clare's faith begin to stir.

Topsy keeps the promise she made while at the side of Eva's deathbed: to be well behaved and committed to learning Christianity from Ophelia. Ophelia has St. Clare sign papers so that she can take Topsy north with her and free her, and she asks him to immediately make provisions for the other slaves. He agrees, but before he is able to do so, is stabbed while trying to break up a fight between two intoxicated men at a café. St. Clare dies at home, and the slaves now belong to Marie, who has no intention of freeing them. Marie decides to sell all the slaves and Ophelia tells her that both her husband's and her daughter's dying wishes were to give Tom his freedom. Marie dismisses this, believing that slaves are better off with masters than free, and that most masters are kind.

At the slave warehouse, where Marie has sent the slaves, a mother named Susan worries that her daughter, Emmeline, will be sold away from her into sexual slavery. Emmeline is a beautiful young girl with gorgeous curly hair and Susan straightens it to make her less attractive before the sale—but the seller forces her to curl it so that she will fetch more money at auction. Susan is separated from her daughter, as her new master cannot afford both of them. Emmeline, along with Tom, are sold to a plantation owner named Simon Legree.

Legree takes Tom in chains and loads him and the other slaves onto a boat, where he strips Tom of all his possessions except the Bible Tom has hidden. Legree tells him that slaves are not allowed to have religion on his plantation, and Tom remains submissive even though in his heart he rejects what Legree is saying. In the wagon on the way to the cotton plantation, Legree gets drunk and makes sexual advances at Emmeline, who is repulsed by him. Legree lives alone at the plantation and proves to be a cruel master, and the community of slaves that lives there is unfriendly compared to what Tom had experienced elsewhere. The two black overseers, Sambo and Quimbo, have been trained in "savageness and brutality" by

Black slaves, both male and female, were forced to perform hard labor in the cotton fields of Southern plantations.

Legree and lord their power over the lower slaves. Tom begins to lose faith, but has a vision of Eva that gives him strength.

Tom goes to work in the cotton fields and meets a woman named Cassy, who was once Legree's female slave of choice and has been replaced by the younger Emmeline. Tom helps a woman who is weak and struggling to complete her work. Cassy warns that once he has spent enough time on the plantation, he won't want to help anyone. When Legree finds out from Sambo and Quimbo that Tom was helping the woman, Legree decides that Tom should be the one to whip her. Tom refuses and is beaten mercilessly by Legree. Despite the vicious attack, Tom rejects Legree's claim to his soul, and Legree orders his overseers to give Tom "a breakin' in."

Cassy comes to tend to Tom's wounds and tells him her story. The daughter of a white man and a slave woman, Cassy was purchased by a lawyer after her father's death and became his mistress. She had a son and a daughter by him and lived happily until he fell in love with another woman. He sold Cassy and her children to a man who wanted Cassy for himself, and her new master soon sold both her children away from her. Purchased by a new master, she had another child, but poisoned the infant rather than have another child grow up to be bought and sold. Eventually, Legree bought Cassy and made her his mistress.

Legree's cruelty was inherited from his father, but his mother was a deeply religious and loving woman. She forgave Legree for all his wrongs in a letter written as she was dying and enclosed a lock of her hair—the same token that Eva gave to her loved ones before she died. Seeing the lock of Eva's hair that Sambo had taken from Tom disturbs Legree, who tries to drown his feelings in liquor. He sees an apparition as he listens to the hymns of the slaves and it terrifies him. He turns his fear into violence against Tom, determined to break him both body and soul, but Tom's faith does not waver. When Cassy tries to get Tom to escape, he refuses, telling her that it is his moral duty to stay and help the "poor souls" at the plantation.

Cassy and Emmeline hatch their escape plan. Playing on Legree's fear of the supernatural, Cassy convinces him that part of the house is haunted. She proceeds to escape with Emmeline and then they return to the house and hide in the "haunted" garret until the search for them is called off and it is safe for them to sneak away. Legree is convinced that Tom knew about their escape plan and threatens his life. But Tom refuses to say a word. Legree beats him within an inch of his life, but Tom, in his martyrdom, forgives Legree. After Legree leaves the overseers to finish the job, Tom prays for Sambo and Quimbo. The "two savage men" weep seeing the error of their ways.

The cruel Simon Legree purchased Tom at auction.

Tom is on the verge of death when George Shelby arrives at the plantation. Tom dies happily and peacefully, filled with Christ's love, with George at his bedside. Filled with anger, George tells Legree he will have him arrested for murder but George has no power since "in all Southern courts, the testimony of colored blood is nothing." After burying Tom, George pledges to dedicate his life to the abolition of slavery.

Cassy and Emmeline successfully escape from Legree and take a boat north to Canada. George Shelby is on the same boat and has a conversation with a former slave named Madame de Thoux. The woman realizes that George Harris is her brother and Cassy, who was listening, believes that Eliza Harris is her long lost daughter. When they reach Montreal, where George and Eliza are living, there is a joyful family reunion. They will ultimately leave Canada for the African nation of Liberia, which is populated by freed slaves.

When George gets home, he frees all the slaves on the Shelby plantation. However, they do not want to leave, so he pays them for their work. He tells everyone of Tom's death and asks that, when they see Uncle Tom's cabin, that they remember their freedom and act as he would.

Cultural Context

At a time of national conflict, both political and cultural, over the issue of slavery, *Uncle Tom's Cabin* was Stowe's call to arms to the everyday reader. By taking a religious approach to the horrors of human bondage, Stowe took the slavery question out of the political sphere and into the parlor. The sectional conflict between the North and South, which was especially tense after the passage of the Fugitive Slave Act, is presented as a moral issue, and Stowe forced her audience to examine their own moral code. At a time when many people had deeply held racial prejudices and considered African Americans to be subhuman, Stowe gives humanity and emotion to her slave characters. She presents their struggles and desires for family, freedom, and equality in a way that white readers could relate to—as mothers, as Christians, and as democratic Americans. The nation was still quite young at the time of publication, and Stowe appeals to an America that had recently fought for its own freedom.

For Harriet, the cruelest aspect of slavery was the act of selling children away from their mothers.

As a woman, Stowe was in a complicated position. It was not yet acceptable for women to speak out on matters considered political or economic, and writing was one of the only ways women could publicly express their opinions. Stowe, who was in many ways a traditional nineteenth century woman, used her position in the female sphere—the domestic and religious influence of the wife and mother—to examine the immoral aspects of slavery that were commonly ignored. To Stowe, the most repugnant part of slavery was the practice of breaking up families by selling them off to different masters, especially the act of taking a child from its mother. At a time when many families, regardless of race or social status, had lost at least one child, Stowe was able to elicit an emotional response from women who could relate to the pain and helplessness that a slave mother must have felt when her child was sold away from her.

Major Characters

Uncle Tom

Tom is a devoutly religious slave who is sold "downriver" by Arthur Shelby and ends up with the ruthless Simon Legree. Tom refuses to be dishonest in any way, refusing to flee and going submissively when he is sold away from his wife and children. Even during the most horrible circumstances, Tom finds strength in God. His faith is tested many times, but he is always able to forgive his persecutors. He dies a martyr's death after a brutal whipping by Legree, and inspires many who knew him to live a good, Christian life.

George and Eliza Harris

George and Eliza are fugitive slaves who make their way north from Kentucky to Canada. George flees when his master plans to marry him off to another woman. Eliza escapes before her son, Harry, is sold away from her. George is willing to do anything for his freedom while Eliza—although an honest and devout woman—cannot bear to be separated from her son. Quakers on the Underground Railroad help the Harrises along, and their kindness gives George faith in God. George, Eliza, and Harry achieve their freedom in Canada and eventually settle in Liberia. George, who is intelligent and resourceful, represents the capacity for those trapped in bondage to thrive outside the institution of slavery. Eliza is the epitome of motherhood, and is meant to evoke feelings of sympathy from white readers who can relate to a mother's love and the loss of a child.

Arthur and Emily Shelby

Arthur Shelby is a Kentucky plantation owner who is kind to his slaves. Despite this humanity, economic circumstances force him to sell Tom and Harry, who is Eliza's son, away from their families. His wife, Emily, attempts to be the voice of morality and pleads with him that it is unchristian to break up a family, although she is powerless to stop it. Emily is one of the novel's many mother figures who appeal to the consciences of their husbands in attempts to fight slavery. Arthur (like Augustine St. Clare later on) represents the "kind master" figure and is meant to appeal to Southern slave owners who feel trapped in a system they know is immoral.

Eva St. Clare

Eva is the young daughter of Augustine and Marie St. Clare, who purchase Tom after he saves Eva's life. Eva is an extremely pious child and shows kindness to all people, black or white. She grows very close to Tom, with whom she shares the same level of religious conviction. Eva is deeply disturbed by slavery and believes that everyone is equal in the eyes of God. She grows ill and dies after making her father promise to free all the slaves. Like Tom, Eva is a Christ-like figure, and through her age and childish innocence Stowe is able to express more radical views about abolition and racial equality.

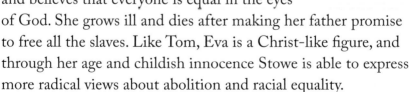

Miss Ophelia

Ophelia, cousin of Augustine St. Clare, is the novel's traditional Northern woman. Hailing from New England, she is against

Eva shared a religious conviction with Tom, and read the Bible to him.

the institution of slavery but is prejudiced against African Americans. Conversations with her cousin and witnessing Eva's kindness force Ophelia to confront her own hypocrisy, and she ends up taking responsibility for the education and freedom of a slave girl, Topsy. The character of Ophelia is meant to speak to Northern Christian readers who maintain racial prejudice while advocating the abolition of slavery.

Simon Legree

Legree is a cruel plantation owner who treats his slaves as subhuman brutes. He is almost completely devoid of humanity (with the exception of his fondness for his dead mother) and does not allow his slaves to practice religion. When he is unable to break Tom of his faith, he whips him to death. Legree is the

The Civil War brought the battle over slavery close to home for those living in the border states.

novel's most immoral character—he is godless and indulges in vices such as drinking and sexual relationships with his female slaves. He represents the worst kind of person that the institution of slavery fosters.

Major Theme: Slavery as a Moral Evil

In *Uncle Tom's Cabin*, Stowe appeals to her readers' moral conscience. In the nineteenth century, Christianity was the dominant religion in America and the novel's moral code is based on Christian values. At a time when slaves were considered property and not people, Stowe shows the slaves' humanity and forces the reader to acknowledge that they share the same emotions and desires—the right to life and liberty, the sanctity of family, and the freedom to worship God.

Stowe uses pious female characters such as Mrs. Bird and the Quaker women to demonstrate that slavery is incompatible with the Christian faith as it violates the Golden Rule, which states that one should do unto others as they would have others do unto them. Throughout the novel, Stowe demonstrates that supporters of slavery in any form cannot call themselves true Christians, since the truly pious should practice charity and love for all God's creatures.

The evils of slavery are depicted even under supposedly kind masters such as Arthur Shelby and Augustine St. Clare. Shelby is a humane man, but sells his slaves out of economic necessity. St. Clare pledges to free Tom and the slaves at Eva's request, but his untimely death allows his cruel wife, Marie, to do with them as she pleases. All the horrors of slavery come together in Simon Legree, who brutalizes his male slaves and sexualizes his female slaves. Stowe works to dispel all the proslavery arguments that slaves are better off under the control of masters than they are free, for no matter how well the slaves are treated, they are still slaves and have no power over their own lives.

Major Symbol: The Ohio River

The Ohio River forms the border between the free state of Ohio and the slave state of Kentucky. In the text it is used as both a physical and symbolic line between slavery and freedom.

For example, when Eliza leaps across the icy river, it is a symbolic crossing—though she is not yet out of danger due to the Fugitive Slave Law, she has made it to the free states of the North.

The Ohio River is often compared to the biblical River Jordan. In the Bible, the Israelites, who had been slaves in Egypt, are led out of bondage and cross the River Jordan into the Promised Land. When Sam returns to the Shelby plantation to tell everyone of Eliza's escape, he says, "she's clar 'cross Jordan. As a body may say, in the land o' Canaan." Many of the hymns and spirituals sung by the slaves incorporate "'Jordan's banks,' and 'Canaan's fields'" and Tom sings to Eva "such beautiful things about the New Jerusalem, and bright angels, and the land of Canaan." The Ohio River, like the biblical River Jordan, is symbolic of the barrier between enslavement and liberty. Crossing it represents the arrival in the Promised Land of freedom outside the slave states.

Stowe (seated, center) is photographed with a group of abolitionist women, circa 1865.

FOUR

A Key to Uncle Tom's Cabin

ublished in 1854, *A Key to Uncle Tom's Cabin: Presenting
the Original Facts and Documents* is Stowe's response to
the harsh criticism she received after the publication of
Uncle Tom's Cabin. *Key* presents a "mosaic of facts" to back up
Stowe's fictional portrayal of American slavery. She includes
excerpts from the slave narratives of Frederick Douglass,
Josiah Henson, and Solomon Northup, and eyewitness accounts
provided in letters from her brother Charles during his three
years in New Orleans, among other forms of documentation to
back up the controversial claims made in her novel. A selection
of some of the most important primary source material from
Key illustrates Stowe's commitment to a realistic portrayal of
slavery. Yet the book is also problematic as it demonstrates
many of Stowe's own prejudices, as well as the larger issue of
whites appropriating and profiting from black slave narratives.

Although *Key* provides a wealth of documentation to back
up Stowe's story, one must consider her social position as a
nineteenth century white woman from a prominent family:

she was viewing the information through a veil of her own prejudices and privilege, and she used it to fit her purposes. The Stowe family relied on Harriet's income, and it was in her best interest to write a book that would entertain and turn a profit. In the opening chapter of *Key*, Stowe admits, "the book is a very inadequate representation of slavery… [which] is too dreadful for the purposes of art" and that "all works which ever mean to give pleasure must draw a veil somewhere, or they cannot succeed." In order to appease her mostly white readership, and ensure that the book would sell, Stowe chose to exclude the worst aspects of slavery. She countered the unpleasantness with moments of comic relief, most notably in the character of the unruly slave child Topsy. Stowe's views on racial equality were quite radical in the nineteenth century, but from a twenty-first century perspective, *Key* provides concrete evidence of cultural appropriation and white ownership of black source material. Additionally, it holds a number of racial stereotypes that *Uncle Tom's Cabin* perpetuated—and which still exist today.

Frederick Douglass and George Harris

In Part One of *Key*, Stowe presents evidence specific to the characters in her novel. In the section on George Harris (Chapter Four), she provides details from Frederick Douglass' autobiography, *Narrative of the Life of Frederick Douglass* (1845), to support her characterization of George as an exceptionally intelligent man who taught himself to read and write. When Douglass was living as a house servant in Baltimore, his mistress, Sophia Auld, began to teach him to read. Douglass' master, Hugh Auld, forced his wife to stop because he believed that the education of slaves made them unmanageable. Douglass then taught himself in secret. At around twelve years old, he built on the basic knowledge of the alphabet that Mrs. Auld had already taught him and enlisted the help of poor

Stowe borrowed heavily from black abolitionist Frederick Douglass' personal narrative to create the character of George Harris.

white children, with whom he traded bread for knowledge. He began to read abolitionist writings and became more and more determined to have his freedom. Douglass learned to write a few letters by watching men at the shipyards, tricking white boys into writing contests, and copying from his young master Thomas' schoolbooks.

Stowe had written a letter to Frederick Douglass in 1851 asking him for help finding firsthand accounts of slaves who had worked on a cotton plantation. She needed source material for the part of *Uncle Tom's Cabin* that takes place at Legree's since she had never been to the Deep South. In this letter she also noted her "regret" at Douglass's position against African colonization and his belief that the church was proslavery.

Despite their differences, the two had a mutual respect for one another and maintained a correspondence. In 1853, Stowe asked Douglass to visit her in Andover shortly before she was scheduled to leave for Britain to receive the Penny Offering. The two discussed what should be done about educating African Americans, and Douglass freely spoke of his desire to build an industrial school where black students could learn practical trades as well as traditional subjects. Stowe supported his position initially, but she changed her mind and did not end up using the money from the Penny Offering for the proposed school. Douglass records his disappointment with Stowe in *The Life and Times of Frederick Douglass* (1881). He also includes a letter he wrote for Stowe to bring to England with her, in which he refutes the idea of colonization: "The truth is, dear madam, we are here, and here we are likely to remain."

It is important to note that, by using Frederick Douglass' narrative as proof of the possibility of George Harris's character, Stowe has taken possession of part of his narrative as her own. Additionally, she has based George Harris—a character who eventually leaves America for Liberia—on a man who was vehemently opposed to the colonization approach to abolition. Frederick Douglass was willing and able to tell his own story in his own words, and he did so quite successfully, yet Stowe still felt she had the right to pick and choose parts of his narrative to suit the needs of her character. This is one of many examples of the way that Stowe believed she had ownership of the slave narrative. Though her stated purpose, as written in a letter to

Former slave Josiah Henson was a pious lay preacher and who served as the basis for the character of Uncle Tom.

the British abolitionist, Lord Denman, was to "speak for the oppressed, who cannot speak for themselves," she took material for her story from those, like Douglass, who very much had their own voice.

Josiah Henson and Uncle Tom

Former slave Josiah Henson (1789–1883) is first mentioned in the chapter on George Harris, where Stowe gives Henson's

91

account of his family being sold at an auction held after his master's death. She provides this to reinforce George Harris' story of being separated from his mother, but most of the information given about Henson comes later, in the chapter on Uncle Tom (Chapter Six). Stowe presents as evidence for Tom's character large portions of Henson's slave narrative, though she summarizes much of it in her own words. The textual evidence she provides directly from Henson's autobiography, *The Life of Josiah Henson* (1849), is used to reinforce Tom's piety and submission in the face of slavery.

The passage that Stowe takes from Henson's narrative is one in which Henson, being transported to New Orleans for sale, is tempted to kill his master and escape. His Christian faith keeps him from taking a life and he realizes that "it was better to die with a Christian's hope... than to live with the incessant recollection of a crime that would destroy the value of life." There are other similarities between Henson and Tom: Henson was a lay preacher to other slaves and an exceedingly honest man, and "no inducements could lead him to feel that it was right for a Christian to violate a pledge solemnly given." Henson is widely regarded as the inspiration for the character of Tom, and he even referred to himself as "Uncle Tom" in the title of his third autobiography. There is a very important difference, however: Henson eventually escaped to freedom in Canada and became a pastor, while his fictional counterpart refused to escape and died at the hands of Legree. Stowe uses Henson's story in her characterization of Tom, but denies Tom the freedom that Henson eventually earned.

In the Uncle Tom chapter of *Key*, Stowe displays the racial prejudice common among the white middle class by ascribing a natural, biologically determined receptiveness to religion and spiritual experiences to black people: "the negro race is confessedly more simple, docile, child-like and affectionate... and hence the divine graces of love and faith... find in their natural temperament a more congenial atmosphere." She goes on to say that the religious vision that comes to Tom can be explained by a psychological difference between the races, where "the negro race... [is] peculiarly susceptible and impressible. Their sensations and impressions are very vivid, and their fancy and imagination lively." Though Stowe advocated for equality, like most nineteenth century whites she believed that there were inherent biological differences between the races, and this prejudice is displayed both in *Uncle Tom's Cabin* and *Key*.

Harriet Jacobs

The most telling example of Stowe's appropriation and perceived ownership of the black slave narrative is a story that does not appear in *Key*, though not for lack of trying on Stowe's part. In 1853, a former slave named Harriet Jacobs wrote to her friend, abolitionist Amy Post, inquiring as to whether she might write to Stowe on her behalf. Jacobs wanted to write her story and was looking for advice on how to go about publishing it, and she wrote a sketch of her life for Post to send to Stowe.

At the time, Jacobs was living as a domestic servant in New York, working for Cornelia Grinnell Willis, who had purchased Jacobs and her daughter, Louisa, and emancipated them. Jacobs wanted her daughter to accompany Stowe on her trip to Great Britain as an antislavery activist, and Cornelia Willis also wrote to Stowe on Jacobs' behalf.

Quaker Amy Post held abolitionist meetings at her home in Rochester, New York.

Former slave Harriet Jacobs contacted Stowe for help with her personal memoir.

When Stowe replied to Mrs. Willis, she both refused to take Louisa and asked her to verify the details of Jacobs' story so she could use it in *Key*. She enclosed the sketch of Jacobs' life that she had received from Amy Post, much to Jacobs' embarrassment, as she had never revealed to Mrs. Willis that her children's father was a prominent white man with whom she had a consensual relationship. Jacobs wrote to Amy Post about her intent to write her own story after receiving Stowe's response: "I wished it to be a history of my life entirely by its s[e]lf which would do more good and it needed no romance." Jacobs politely declined to allow Stowe to use her story for *Key*, but offered to give her any factual details about slavery that might be useful to her. Stowe did not answer any subsequent letters from Jacobs or Mrs. Willis, nor did she aid Jacobs in the publication of her memoir. Ultimately, Harriet Jacobs wrote her own story and *Incidents in the Life of a Slave Girl* was published in 1861 under the pseudonym Linda Brent.

Timeline

1811 Harriet Beecher Stowe is born on June 14, in Litchfield, Connecticut, to Lyman Beecher and Roxana Foote Beecher.

1816 American Colonization Society is established; Roxana Foote Beecher dies.

1820 Missouri Compromise establishes 36°30′ latitude line to determine whether states would be admitted to the Union as slave or free.

1824 Harriet Beecher enters Hartford Female Seminary, founded by her eldest sister, Catharine Beecher.

1826 Sojourner Truth escapes slavery.

1831 Nat Turner leads slave rebellion; William Lloyd Garrison begins publishing *The Liberator*.

1832 The Beechers move to Cincinnati, Ohio, where Lyman Beecher takes a position at the Lane Theological Seminary.

1833 The American Anti-Slavery Society is established; Harriet visits a Kentucky plantation owned by a family friend; *Primary Geography for Children* becomes Harriet's first published work; Harriet is invited to join the Semi-Colon Club; Great Britain abolishes slavery.

1834 Harriet's first published work of fiction, "A New England Sketch," appears in *Western Monthly Magazine*; the Lane Debates over immediate emancipation cause controversy between students and trustees.

1836 Harriet Beecher marries Calvin Stowe and gives birth to twin daughters, Eliza and Hattie; the House of Representatives enacts a gag rule on antislavery petitions; mob violence erupts in Cincinnati and James G. Birney's abolitionist press is destroyed.

1838 Frederick Douglass escapes slavery and becomes active in the abolitionist movement; Henry Ellis Stowe is born.

1839 The Stowes employ a former slave and help her escape to freedom when her former master comes to reclaim her.

1840 American and Foreign Anti-Slavery Society is established; Frederick William Stowe is born.

1843 Georgiana May Stowe is born; Harriet's brother, George Beecher, dies of a (possibly self-inflicted) gunshot wound.

1844 Harriet witnesses a family torn apart at a slave auction on a Kentucky plantation.

1845 Texas is annexed by the United States and admitted into the Union; Harriet falls ill with cholera; "Immediate Emancipation" appears in the *New-York Evangelist*.

1846 Wilmot Proviso passes the House but not the Senate.

1848 Treaty of Guadalupe Hidalgo ends the Mexican-American War and the United States acquires the Mexican Cession territory; Samuel Charles Stowe is born.

1849 Harriet's infant son, Samuel, dies of cholera.

Timeline

1850 The Compromise of 1850 makes it mandatory for Northerners to return escaped slaves under the Fugitive Slave Act; the Beechers become active in the Underground Railroad; the Stowes move to Brunswick, Maine; "The Freeman's Dream" is published in the *National Era*.

1851–1852 *Uncle Tom's Cabin* appears in serial form in the *National Era* and is published in book form in 1852.

1853 *A Key to Uncle Tom's Cabin* is published; the Stowes move to Andover, Massachusetts, and travel to Europe for a speaking tour.

1854 The Kansas-Nebraska Act is passed, leaving the question of slavery in the territories to popular sovereignty and sparking a period of violence known as "Bleeding Kansas"; *Sunny Memories of Foreign Lands* is published.

1856 Beecher Stowe publishes *Dred: A Tale of the Great Dismal Swamp*; John Brown leads massacre in the Pottawatomie Creek area of Kansas.

1857 U.S. Supreme Court renders Dred Scott decision; Henry Ellis Stowe dies by accidental drowning.

1858 Lincoln delivers his "House Divided" speech; the Lincoln-Douglas debates argue the slavery question.

1859 John Brown raids Harpers Ferry, Virginia, in a failed attempt to incite rebellion; *The Minister's Wooing* is published.

1860 Abraham Lincoln is elected as the sixteenth president of the Unites States; seven Southern states secede from the Union.

1861 The Civil War begins after the attack on Fort Sumter in Charleston Harbor; Harriet's son, Frederick, enlists in the Union army.

1862 Harriet meets President Lincoln at the White House.

1863 Lincoln issues the Emancipation Proclamation; Lyman Beecher dies; Frederick William Stowe is injured at the Battle of Gettysburg and becomes dependent on alcohol.

1865 The Civil War ends in Union victory; the Thirteenth Amendment abolishes slavery; the Stowes purchase land in Florida.

1868 The Fourteenth Amendment makes former slaves American citizens.

1870 The Fifteenth Amendment grants voting rights to black men; Frederick William Stowe disappears after boarding a ship in San Francisco and is presumed dead; *Lady Byron Vindicated* is published; Henry Ward Beecher is publicly accused of adultery.

1886 Calvin Stowe dies.

1887 Harriet's daughter Georgiana dies; Harriet's brother, Henry Ward Beecher dies; Harriet begins to exhibit signs of dementia.

1896 Harriet Beecher Stowe dies in her Hartford, Connecticut, home.

Stowe's Most Important Works

Fiction

The Mayflower (1843)

"Immediate Emancipation" (1845)

"The Freeman's Dream" (1850)

Uncle Tom's Cabin (1852)

Sunny Memories of Foreign Lands (1854)

Dred: A Tale of the Great Dismal Swap (1856)

The Minister's Wooing (1859)

Agnes of Sorrento (1862)

Oldtown Folks (1869)

Pink and White Tyranny (1871)

Oldtown Fireside Stories (1872)

Poganuc People (1878)

Nonfiction

Primary Geography for Children (1833), with Catharine Beecher

A Key to Uncle Tom's Cabin (1854)

"An Appeal to the Women of the Free States of America, On the Present Crisis in Our Country" (1854)

"The Reply" (1863)

Lady Byron Vindicated (1870)

Glossary

annexation
The incorporation of new territory into an existing political unit such as a country, state, county, or city.

appropriations
An act of a legislature authorizing money to be paid from the treasury for a specified use.

calisthenics
Gymnastic exercises designed to develop muscular tone and promote physical well-being.

Calvinism
A Christian theology stressing the depravity of humans (who are born sinners), the sovereignty of God, the doctrine of predestination, and the supreme authority of the Scriptures.

cholera
An infectious and often fatal bacterial disease of the small intestine, typically contracted from infected water supplies and causing severe vomiting and diarrhea.

daguerreotype
An old type of photograph that was made on a piece of silver or a piece of copper covered in silver.

egalitarian
The principle that all people are equal and deserve equal rights and opportunities.

Glossary

manifest destiny
The nineteenth-century belief that the expansion of the United States throughout North America was both justified and inevitable.

manumission
The act of freeing slaves.

mulatto
Outdated term for a person of mixed white and black ancestry, especially a person with one white and one black parent.

omnibus bill
A piece of legislation that includes a number of miscellaneous provisions or appropriations in a single package.

parable
A short, fictional story that teaches a moral or spiritual lesson.

perfectionism
A belief in certain religions that moral or spiritual perfection can be achieved before the soul has passed into the afterlife.

postmillennialism
The Protestant theological belief that the second coming of Christ will follow the millennium.

predestination
The belief that everything that will happen has already been determined by God and cannot be changed.

pseudonym
A name that someone (such as a writer) uses instead of his or her real name.

scrupulous
Having a conscience that is overly self critical.

sentimentalism
A literary style, popular in the nineteenth century, which uses the excessive expression of feelings of tenderness, sadness, and nostalgia to elicit a strong emotional response from the reader.

temperance
The practice of abstaining from alcohol or drinking moderately.

tuberculosis
An infectious bacterial disease mainly affecting the lungs.

Sources

Introduction

P. 9: Harriet Beecher Stowe Center, The, "The National and International Impact of Uncle Tom's Cabin," www.harriet-beecherstowecenter.org/utc/impact.shtml.

Chapter 1

P. 19: PBS, "This Far By Faith: Sojourner Truth," www.pbs.org/thisfarbyfaith/people/sojourner_truth.html.

P. 31: Abraham Lincoln, "A House Divided" Speech, Springfield, Illinois, June 16, 1858, millercenter.org/scripps/archive/speeches/detail/3504.

Chapter 2

P. 37: Joan D. Hedrick, *Harriet Beecher Stowe: A Life* (New York, NY: Oxford University Press, 1994), p. 32.

P. 39: Joan D. Hedrick, *Harriet Beecher Stowe: A Life*, p. 68.

P. 45: Joan D. Hedrick, *Harriet Beecher Stowe: A Life*, p. 121.

P. 52: The Harriet Beecher Stowe Center, "The National and International Impact of Uncle Tom's Cabin," www.harriet-beecherstowecenter.org/utc/impact.shtml.

Chapter 3

All quotations from *Uncle Tom's Cabin* are from the 2005 Dover Thrift edition.

Chapter 4

P. 90: All quotations from *A Key to Uncle Tom's Cabin* are from the 2008 Applewood Books edition.

P. 91: Belasco, Susan, ed., "Frederick Douglass, Letter to Harriet Beecher Stowe, March 8, 1853," in *Stowe In Her Own Time* (Iowa City, IA: University of Iowa Press, 2009), p. 90.

P. 91: Joan D. Hedrick, *Harriet Beecher Stowe: A Life*, p. 249.

P. 94: Belasco, Susan, ed., "Harriet Jacobs, Letter to Amy Post, April 4, 1853," in *Stowe In Her Own Time*, p. 100.

Further Information

Books

Ammons, Elizabeth, ed. *Harriet Beecher Stowe's Uncle Tom's Cabin: A Casebook*. New York, NY: Oxford University Press, 2007.

Ferrel, Claudine L. *The Abolitionist Movement*. Westport, CT: Greenwood Press, 2006.

Lowance, Mason, ed. *Against Slavery: An Abolitionist Reader*. New York, NY: Penguin Classics, 2000.

Sonneborn, Liz. *Harriet Beecher Stowe*. New York, NY: Chelsea House, 2009.

Websites

Digital History: Pre-Civil War Era

www.digitalhistory.uh.edu/era.cfm?eraID=5&smtid=2

Conduct research, analyze primary sources, and draw your own conclusions about pre-Civil War history through the Digital History explorations page.

Digital History: Slavery

www.digitalhistory.uh.edu/era.cfm?eraID=6&smtid=2

Explore slavery's origins, the definitions of slavery, and its impact on American culture, economics, and politics.

The Harriet Beecher Stowe Center

www.harrietbeecherstowecenter.org

Learn more about Stowe's life, education, and her family. Also discover a wide selection of titles relating to Women's Studies, social justice, African American Studies, the Civil War, abolition, and slavery.

Bibliography

Ammons, Elizabeth, ed. *Harriet Beecher Stowe's Uncle Tom's Cabin: A Casebook*. New York, NY: Oxford University Press, 2007.

Belasco, Susan, ed. *Stowe in Her Own Time*. Iowa City, IA: University of Iowa Press, 2009.

Boydston, Jeanne, Mary Kelley, and Anne Margolis. *The Limits of Sisterhood: The Beecher Sisters on Women's Rights and Woman's Sphere*. Chapel Hill, NC: University of North Carolina Press, 1988.

Ferrel, Claudine L. *The Abolitionist Movement*. Westport, CT: Greenwood Press, 2006.

Goldner, Ellen J. "Arguing with Pictures: Race, Class, and the Formation of Popular Abolitionism through *Uncle Tom's Cabin*." Journal of American & Comparative Cultures 24, no. 1/2 (2001): 71–84.

Hedrick, Joan D. *Harriet Beecher Stowe: A Life*. New York, NY: Oxford University Press, 1994.

Potter, David M. *The Impending Crisis: America Before the Civil War*. New York, NY: Harper Perennial, 2011.

Reynolds, David S. *Mightier Than the Sword: Uncle Tom's Cabin and the Battle for America*. New York, NY: W.W. Norton & Company, 2011.

Stowe, Harriet Beecher. *A Key to Uncle Tom's Cabin*. Bedford, MA: Applewood Books, 2008.

Stowe, Harriet Beecher. *The Oxford Harriet Beecher Stowe Reader*. Edited by Joan D. Hedrick. New York, NY: Oxford University Press, 1999.

Stowe, Harriet Beecher. *Uncle Tom's Cabin*. New York, NY: Dover Publications, 2005.

Index

About the Author

Alison Morretta holds a Bachelor of Arts in English and Creative Writing from Kenyon College in Gambier, Ohio, where she studied the literature and history of antebellum America. She has worked in book publishing since 2005, developing and copyediting both fiction and nonfiction manuscripts. Alison lives in New York City with her loving husband, Bart, and their rambunctious Corgi, Cassidy. Morretta's other titles in this series include *F. Scott Fitzgerald and the Jazz Age* and *John Steinbeck and the Great Depression*.